Rationality
and Religious
Experience

To Mary:

May This little work help
in advancing cross-cultural understanding.
With best wishes

Henry Rosemont Jr

April, '03

Rationality and Religious Experience

The Continuing Relevance of the World's Spiritual Traditions

HENRY ROSEMONT, Jr.

With a Commentary by
Huston Smith

*Followed by a Response, Discussion,
and Epilogue*

The First Master Hsüan Hua
Memorial Lecture

OPEN COURT
Chicago and La Salle, Illinois

To order books from Open Court, call 1-800-815-2280.

Open Court Publishing Company is a division of Carus Publishing Company.

Printed and bound in the United States of America.

Library of Congress Cataloging-in-Publication Data

Rosemont, Henry, 1934–
    Rationality and religious experience : the continuing relevance of the world's spiritual traditions / Henry Rosemont, Jr. ; with a commentary by Huston Smith.
       p. cm. — (The Master Hsüan Hua memorial lecture ; 1)
    Includes bibliographical references and index.
    ISBN 0-8126-9446-5 (alk. paper)
    1. Religions.   I. Title.   II. Series.

BL74.R67 2001
200—dc21

                                  2001036544

This book includes the text of a lecture sponsored by the Institute for World Religions, the Graduate Theological Union, and The Center for Chinese Studies of the University of California at Berkeley, April 7, 2000.

CONTENTS

THE FIRST HSÜAN HUA MEMORIAL LECTURE

*T*he Institute for World Religions, in partnership with
the Asian Pacific Rim Working Group of the Graduate
Theological Union, and in conjunction with the Center
for Chinese Studies/East Asian Studies Center of the
University of California at Berkeley, sponsored the first
annual Venerable Hsüan Hua Memorial Lecture, held
Friday, April 7, 2000 at 7:00 P.M. in the Memorial
Chapel of the Pacific School of Religion, Berkeley.
This new lectureship focuses on bringing the ancient
wisdom of Asian religions and philosophy to bear on
the pressing issues of the modern world, especially in
the area of ethics and spiritual values.

The first Hsüan Hua Memorial Lecture, originally
entitled "Whither the World's Religions?," was given
by Henry Rosemont, Jr., who holds an Honors A.B.
from the University of Illinois, Ph.D. in Philosophy
from the University of Washington, and has pursued
post-doctoral studies in Linguistics at M.I.T., and in
Advanced Chinese Studies at the University of
London. He is the author of *A Chinese Mirror* (1991),

the forthcoming *Confucian Alternatives* (2002), and over seventy articles in scholarly journals and anthologies. He has edited and/or translated seven other works, the most recent of which, with Roger T. Ames, is a translation of *The Analects of Confucius* (1998). Rosemont was Book Review Editor of *Philosophy East and West* from 1972 to 1988; President of the Society for Asian and Comparative Philosophy 1976–1978, and is currently editor of the Society's Monograph Series. The recipient of fellowships from the NEH, ACLS, NSF, and the Fulbright Program, Dr. Rosemont is currently George B. and Willma Reeves Distinguished Professor of the Liberal Arts at St. Mary's College of Maryland, Senior Consulting Professor at Fudan University in Shanghai, and Professorial Lecturer at the School of Advanced International Studies of The Johns Hopkins University.

A lengthy response and discussion followed Dr. Rosemont's lecture, begun by Huston Smith (Professor Emeritus, University of California at Berkeley), author of *The Religions of Man* (1958) and *The World's Religions* (1989). Professor Smith, a leading figure in the comparative philosophy of religion, is widely regarded as the most eloquent and accessible contemporary authority on the history and philosophy of religions. The lecture was open to the general public.

A BRIEF PORTRAIT
OF THE VENERABLE MASTER
HSÜAN HUA

"*I* have had many names," he once said, "and all
of them are false." In his youth in Manchuria, he was
known as "the Filial Son Bai"; as a young monk he
was An Tzu ("Peace and Kindness"); later, in Hong
Kong, he was Tu Lun ("Wheel of Rescue"); finally,
in America, he was Hsüan Hua, which might be
translated as "one who proclaims the principles of
transformation." To his thousands of disciples across
the world, he was always also "Shr Fu" —"Teacher."

Born in 1918 into a peasant family in a small
village on the Manchurian plain, Master Hua was the
youngest of ten children. He attended school for only
two years, during which he studied the Chinese
classics and committed many of them to memory.
As a young teenager, he opened a free school for both
children and adults. He also began then one of his
lifelong spiritual practices: reverential bowing.
Outdoors, in all weather, he would make over 800
prostrations daily, as a profound gesture of his respect
for all that is good and sacred in the universe.

He was nineteen when his mother died, and for three years he honored her memory by sitting in meditation in a hut beside her grave. It was during this time that he made a resolve to go to America to teach the principles of wisdom. As a first step, at the end of the period of mourning, he entered San Yuan Monastery, took as his teacher Master Chang Chih, and subsequently received the full ordination of a Buddhist monk at Pu To Mountain. For ten years he devoted himself to study of the Buddhist scriptural tradition and to mastery of both the Esoteric and the Ch'an Schools of Chinese Buddhism. He had also read and contemplated the scriptures of Christianity, Daoism, and Islam. Thus, by the age of thirty, he had already established through his own experience the four major imperatives of his later ministry in America: the primacy of the monastic tradition; the duty to educate; the need for Buddhists to ground themselves in traditional spiritual practice and authentic scripture; and, just as essential, the importance and the power of ecumenical respect and understanding.

In 1948, Master Hua traveled south to meet the Venerable Hsu Yun, who was then already 108 years old and China's most distinguished spiritual teacher. From him Master Hua received the patriarchal transmission in the Wei Yang Lineage of the Ch'an School. Master Hua subsequently left China for Hong Kong. He spent a dozen years there, first in seclusion, then later as a teacher at three monasteries that he founded.

Finally, in 1962, several of his Hong Kong disciples invited him to come to San Francisco. By 1968, Master Hua had established the Buddhist Lecture Hall in a loft in San Francisco's Chinatown, and there he began giving nightly lectures, in Chinese, to an audience of young Americans. His texts were the major scriptures of the Mahayana. In 1969, he astonished the monastic community of Taiwan by sending there, for final ordination, two American women and three American men, all five of them fully trained as novices, fluent in Chinese, and conversant with Buddhist scripture. During subsequent years, the Master trained and oversaw the ordination of hundreds of monks and nuns who came to California to study with him from all over North America, as well as from Europe, Australia, and Asia. These monastic disciples now teach in the twenty-eight temples, monasteries, and convents that the Master founded in the United States, Canada, and several Asian countries. The City of Ten Thousand Buddhas, located in California's North Coast 100 miles north of San Francisco, is home to over two hundred Buddhist monks and nuns, making it the largest Buddhist monastic community in North America.

Although he understood English well and spoke it when it was necessary, Master Hua almost always lectured in Chinese. His aim was to encourage Westerners to learn Chinese, so that they could become translators, not merely of his lectures, but of the major scriptural texts of the Buddhist Mahayana. His intent was realized. So far, the Buddhist Text Translation Society, which he founded, has issued over 130 volumes of translation of the major Sutras, together with a similar number of commentaries, instructions, and stories from the Master's teaching.

As an educator, Master Hua was tireless. From 1968 to the mid-1980s he gave as many as a dozen lectures a week, and he traveled extensively on speaking tours. He also established formal training programs for monastics and for laity; elementary and secondary schools for boys and for girls; Dharma Realm Buddhist University at the City of Ten Thousand Buddhas; and the Institute for World Religions, in Berkeley.

Throughout his life the Master taught that the basis of spiritual practice is moral practice. Of his monastic disciples he required strict purity, and he encouraged his lay disciples to adhere to the five precepts of the Buddhist laity. Especially in his later years, Confucian texts were often the subject of his lectures, and he held to the Confucian teaching that the first business of education is moral education. He identified six rules of conduct as the basis of communal life at the City of Ten Thousand Buddhas; the six rules prohibited contention, covetousness, self-seeking, selfishness, profiting at the expense of the community, and false speech. He asked that schoolchildren at the City recite these prohibitions every morning before class. In general, although he admired the independent-mindedness of Westerners, he believed that they lacked ethical balance and needed that stabilizing sense of public morality which is characteristic of the East.

The Venerable Master insisted on ecumenical respect, and he delighted in interfaith dialogue. He stressed commonalities in religious traditions—above all their emphasis on proper conduct, on compassion, and on wisdom. He was also a pioneer in building bridges between different Buddhist national traditions; for example, he often brought monks from Theravada countries to California to share the duties of transmitting the precepts of ordination. He invited Catholic priests to celebrate the mass in the Buddha Hall at the City of Ten Thousand Buddhas, and he developed a late-in-life friendship with Paul Cardinal Yu-Bin, the exiled leader of the Catholic Church in China and Taiwan. He once told Cardinal Yu-Bin: "You can be a Buddhist among the Catholics, and I'll be a Catholic among Buddhists." To the Master, the essential teachings of all religions could be summed up in a single word: wisdom.

Master Hua is no longer with us in body. Although he continued to travel and lecture occasionally, he had for the most part retired by the late 1980s. He entered stillness on June 7, 1995. Throughout his life, he had shunned fame, fanfare, and celebrity—he sometimes called himself "the monk with no name"—and in that spirit, his passing was honored with simplicity. Despite his extraordinary legacy and the depth of his influence on thousands of people during his lifetime, his name is, still, little known to the wider public.

PREFACE

*I*T WAS A SIGNAL HONOR to have been invited to give the first Master Hsüan Hua Memorial Lecture, sponsored by the Institute for World Religions, and co-sponsored by the Graduate Theological Union (GTU) and the Center for Chinese/East Asian Studies of the University of California at Berkeley.

I am deeply grateful to the IWR for the invitation, and most especially to Drs. Snjezana Akpinar, Ron Epstein, Martin Verhoeven, Douglas Powers, and Bhikshu Heng Sure for their kindness while I was there, and for their comments on my lecture thereafter.

I was also honored and grateful to have my distinguished colleague and cherished friend Huston Smith offer to make comments on my remarks, and as always, learned much from him.

A first draft of the lecture was given as the annual Reeves Lecture at St. Mary's College of Maryland, and subsequent to its presentation at GTU given again at Chulalongkorn University in Bangkok, Thailand, and as a keynote address at the Annual

Meeting of the Asian Studies Development Program at the East-West Center in Honolulu; I am indebted to these audiences for their comments, insights, and encouragement. A close reading of the text by Professors David Wong of Duke University and Leroy Rouner of Boston University have reduced measurably the number of obscurities found in it. As always, David Ramsey Steele, Editorial Director at Open Court, provided much useful commentary and criticism, as did my editor, Kerri Mommer; I am grateful to them both.

Both the lecture and my responses to questions have been expanded somewhat from the original presentation, and gross infelicities of expression have been deleted from the transcriptions of the tapes of my discussion remarks. As much as possible, however, it was thought best to preserve the integrity of the evening, and consequently I have added an Epilogue which attempts to deal with issues inadequately covered in the lecture and discussion, and I have also provided notes and references to my texts. I hope the resultant narrative is not too disjointed.

Finally, once again I am deeply indebted to Ms. Mary Bloomer of St. Mary's College for turning draft after draft of my handwritten scribbles into a polished and aesthetically pleasing manuscript; poor though my efforts may prove to be, they would be far poorer without her great and always gracious assistance.

Rationality
and Religious
Experience

WE ARE AT THE DAWN NOT ONLY OF A NEW CENTURY, but a new millennium. It is becoming a commonplace—perhaps too common—that in both economics and communications we are on the cusp of becoming a "global village." Normally, however, the term "village" conjures up a vision of a fairly small, cohesive community whose members share at least roughly a common conception of the good, where wealth is not too inequitably distributed, with fresh air and clean water in abundance, and where ethnic distrust and dislike is rare, and violence at a minimum.

Surely this is not a picture of the "global village," and in my view it would be foolish to believe that a capitalist economic system and communications advances could make it a reality. Not only is wealth distributed grossly inequitably today, the gap between rich and poor is widening, not narrowing. And with half of the world's people never having used even a telephone, and far too poor to own one, it is highly unlikely that the Internet and World Wide Web will serve any but the relatively affluent.

I am not an economist, and hence will not say too much about economic justice in a global context. Rather do I want to focus on another area that appears to sharply divide the human race, the world's religions, and the basic claim I will advance is that the many and varied spiritual traditions of the world have a significant potential for enhancing the nonmaterial dimensions of our all-too-human lives, and an equal potential for making this all-too-fragile earth a more peaceful, just, and humane one in the twenty-first century than it was in the twentieth.

This is fundamentally a philosophical claim, and in order to defend it with any hope of endorsement I must also advance a number of others, sufficient in scope and quantity to make arguing for all of them exhaustively distractive from the more general claim. Consequently, while there is philosophical analysis in these pages, the thrust of the work is on synthesis, and I therefore offer apologies at the outset to those whose philosophical sensibilities run in the other direction.[1]

Before proceeding directly to a consideration of my main thesis, however, I must first attempt to respond to two justifiably skeptical questions about it at the outset: *Can* the world's religions have a significant bearing on the lives of people living in a global, postmodern society? And second, *should* they have such a bearing?

That is to say, haven't the physical and life sciences broadened and deepened our understanding of the world we live in to the point where no intelligent person can credit the accounts of that world proffered by religions? And with respect to the second skeptical question, given the manifold horrors human beings have visited on one another in the name of religions, wouldn't humankind be better off without them?

I want to give both of these skeptical questions their just due, in polemic fashion. To elaborate on the first, if one can believe that, troubled by the way some of his creatures were behaving, a Creator of the Universe spoke in flawless Hebrew about His concerns through a burning bush that was not consumed by the flames, then one should have no trouble believing as well that when His flaming lecture and instructions proved inadequate, He later had a son born to him whose major tasks were to speak again, and then suffer and die prematurely in order to bring home the importance of what He was saying.

In the same way, if one can believe such things, one should easily be able to also believe that when the Creator's words again fell on deaf ears, He spoke again; this time in elegant Arabic, to an illiterate shepherd turned merchant.

And the reason why we should believe all of these things if we can believe any one of them is that they equally violate the principles of physics, chemistry, and biology that every rational person accepts today.

I do not wish by these remarks to castigate only the three great religions of the Abrahamic tradition. It no less flies in the face of modern science to believe that the preserver god Vishnu once incarnated himself as Krishna, not merely to give counsel to the spiritual warrior Arjuna, but also, among many other exploits, to make love to 20,000 milkmaids in a single day.

Many popular accounts of Buddhist and Daoist heavens and hells are no less incredible, as are the *kami* of Shinto, the demons of Tibetan Bon, the poison oracles of the Azande in Africa, and the varied creation stories of Native American peoples. (Parenthetical comment: virtually alone among the world's religious traditions, the classical texts of Confucianism contain no statements that contravene physical principles; perhaps that is why some people do not consider Confucianism to be a genuine religious tradition.)

Read literally as descriptions of how the world came to be, what is in it, how it functions, and what its future will be, all of these accounts must, to anyone even minimally knowledgeable about and sympathetic to modern science, be given an equal degree of credence, namely, zero. For all of the events and entities described in these narratives there is no empirical evidence whatsoever beyond the texts themselves, and given that within limits, human beings can individually and collectively shape their future in many different ways, that future cannot be predicted.

No, we cannot accept as factual accounts of the world much that is said and read in sacred narratives. But even though we cannot accept them as such, we can believe that they are all, in one way or another, saying something that is true; statements can be made directly or indirectly, and beliefs about them can take different forms, as can faith.

Let me illustrate this point by citing an example from Huston Smith's *Forgotten Truth*, in which he quotes from an article by the noted physicist Robert Oppenheimer, who wrote:

If we ask whether the electron's position changes with time,
we must say "No,"
If we ask whether the position of the electron remains the same,
we must say "No,"
If we ask whether the electron is at rest,
we must say "No,"
If we ask whether it is in motion,
we must say "No."

Later, Smith continues, the French poet and novelist François Mauriac was shown this article, and asked to comment thereon. After reading it, Mauriac shook his head and said: "What this professor says is far more incredible that what we poor Christians believe."[2]

Now I am not a Christian, but like Mauriac, I, too, find Oppenheimer's statements incredible. I cannot accept them as literal fact, for they violate basic principles of logic and ordinary physics, and contradict the entire testimony of my senses over the course of my lifetime. But in another way, it is not difficult for me to believe there is truth in what Oppenheimer said; clearly he is using these unusual sentences to help us gain a purchase on some very unusual features of the world of quantum mechanics as developed by modern physicists. I will return to this theme of direct and indirect statements and beliefs again, but now want to address briefly the second skeptical question: Given the horrendously large number of pagans, heathens, infidels, atheists, and others who have been slaughtered over the centuries by fanatical adherents of different faiths, why should we want to keep those faiths alive, and attempt to find inspiration in them?

In the ancient world, neither the Egyptians nor the Caananites would have been inclined to pay homage to the God of Israel, with good reason. Christians have persecuted Jews and pagans ever since the Church became powerful enough to do so. Far fewer people would have been killed had Muslims focused more on the spiritual significance of the Hajj, and Ramadan, and less on Jihad. But then the Crusades probably made some Jihads inevitable. As we know from the blood-splattered pages of the history of such events as the Inquisition and the Thirty Years' War, Christians have not been loath to persecute other Christians, easily recognizable as enemies because they were heretics. South Asian Hindus have persecuted South Asian Muslims no less violently, and destroyed more than one mosque. And of course South Asian Muslims have replied in kind. (Another parenthetical comment: The religions of East Asia, and the so-called "minor" religious traditions of indigenous peoples have been much less murderous in this regard.)

In response to this indictment—and it is an indictment—let me suggest the following. First, from the former Yugoslavia to Israel/Palestine to Kashmir, and many other areas in between, religious violence continues to this day, and an antimodern fundamentalism is widespread in many religious traditions. These religions are by no means going to go away, and to argue that they *should* go away is, to my mind, a vacuous intellectual enterprise; the facts of contemporary religious expression must be directly confronted, and the most appropriate counter to the beliefs underlying the more violent of those expressions will almost surely need to come from within the religious traditions whence they have sprung.

A second response to this indictment is that when we look to the spiritual heroes and heroines of the world's faiths, we do not find fanatics eager to behead the unbeliever. On the contrary, sages and saints revered in these traditions—Julian of Norwich, Francis of Assisi, Theresa of Avila, Moses Maimonides, Ibn Khaldoun, Mohandas Gandhi, Gautama the Buddha, Confucius, Lao Zi, Black Elk, and the Dalai Lama, to name only a few—have all proclaimed a common humanity for the world's peoples, and had a profound empathy for human suffering, which they knew to be universal. Political and/or philosophical though some of their works and lives may have been, they are revered both within their own and across religious traditions basically because of their spiritual qualities.

These two responses are intended jointly to suggest that efforts to exorcise religion from the human realm because of the mischief that has been committed in its name is to throw out the baby with the bath water, and equally to suggest a third response, that there is no hope for the cross-cultural dialogues necessary for the creation and maintenance of a more peaceful and just twenty-first century until and unless everyone can come to understand how an intelligent and thoroughly decent human being might come to be, or remain, a subscriber to one or another of the world's faiths. We cannot focus our attention unduly on the most fanatical fundamentalists among them, nor solely on their metaphysical and theological claims.

My final response to the question of whether we should endeavor to keep alive our religious heritages brings me to the heart of my remarks, the claim that the texts we consider sacred when read appropriately, and in conjunction with the sacred texts and narratives of other traditions, can guide us back from the abyss of meaninglessness that is becoming increasingly characteristic of contemporary life, an altogether material life in which many of us are obliged to take jobs we do not like or find satisfying in order to buy things that we do not need and that do not satisfy us either, all the while destroying our natural and social environments as we do so. And even for those of us among the world's peoples who are fortunate enough to lead interesting lives, there is ever less time to reflect on the worthiness and significance of the lives we are leading, and we grow increasingly uncomfortable with the knowledge that much of our material well-being comes at the expense of the poor.

By urging everyone to approach their own text tradition afresh, and alongside others, I am assuming what many of you might find implausible, namely, that in many basic respects all sacred texts are saying the same things, and contain the same truths we can all come to believe without in any way surrendering our rationality.[3]

LET ME BEGIN DEFENDING THIS ASSUMPTION by going back to the beginning, Genesis, a central chapter in all three of the Abrahamic religious traditions. In it, we are told to believe that an omniscient and omnipotent deity created the world and everything in it, in six-sevenths of a time-span, and thereafter took His leisure. As I suggested at the outset, this is fantastic to believe. But the early sections of Genesis are also conveying something else, an assumption implicit in the text and which has been indirectly believed by virtually every inheritor thereof: namely, that the universe is ordered rationally, and is purposeful. Given that we have been created in His image, that is, are rational, it must be that we can come to know what He created, and thereby, perhaps gain insight into the question of why He created it, and most specifically, why He created us to be part of the world.[4]

This indirect belief in the explanatory intelligibility of the world has been, I would argue, of greater significance for the unique manner in which Western civilization has developed than what is supposed to be directly believed as literally described in Genesis.

The history of Western science, for example, has no parallels elsewhere, and if I am right, should be seen, like philosophy, not as competitive with religion, but as one of its children. Not until the so-called Enlightenment did the emphasis begin to shift away from an understanding of nature—God's creation—to a mere manipulation of it. We cannot, I would submit, fully understand what a Copernicus, Kepler, Galileo, or Leibniz was about unless we see each of them as seeking not only astronomical but spiritual understanding as well: the more we learn about the details of *what* He created, the more we may come to a knowledge of the *why* of it.

The patterns of Western education also reveal a deep indebtedness to the Abrahamic affirmation that the universe is explanatorily intelligible, for the dominant thrust of that education has always been to transmit information about the universe: to narrate facts about the world, and construct theories which place those facts in a rational order. Descriptive statements about the way the world is, and functions, are what textbooks contain, statements paraphrased and elaborated upon by teachers. Many facts must be simply memorized—which is why we have true/false and multiple-guess examinations—and we must learn to group facts as well, narrated in essay exams, term papers, and doctoral dissertations.

Briefly combining these remarks about Western science and education, we may come to appreciate better why science is so often seen as hostile to religion, especially if the Abrahamic traditions are seen as paradigmatic of religion. If Genesis is read basically as a description of the way the world came to be, and is, true believers can obviously get in serious trouble taking physics, chemistry, astronomy, geology, or biology courses. "Because Adam needed a proper companion" will not earn a passing grade as a response to any exam questions about female anatomy or gender more generally.

These matters are so central to the Western intellectual tradition that it must appear trivial to raise them. But it is not trivial. Consider India, which has not one, but dozens of creation narratives, each of which is flatly incompatible with the others. Nowhere in the numerous Indian texts is there an affirmation that the universe is explanatorily intelligible. China, on the other hand, has *no* creation stories in its formative literature, which equally contain no affirmation that the universe is explanatorily intelligible.[5]

In both cultures, especially the Chinese, the world is discernible for what it is, through the testimony of the senses, that is, through appearances; even in India these appearances are not generally deceptive,[6] yet the details of the what and the why of the world (that is, the existence of some underlying principles or "stuff" of ultimate reality) do not seem to have preoccupied early Indian and Chinese thinkers. They did not have scriptural or other good reasons for thinking that there might be an explanation of why the world is ultimately as it is, and thereby had no reason for seeking an answer, transcendental or otherwise, to the question of why we are in this world; this is uniquely Western, and Abrahamic.

If this claim is warranted, it suggests that we should read the sacred texts of India and China in a different way: From Krishna to Confucius, the ancient sages of Asia should be construed not merely as basically giving us descriptions of a world uniquely created for some rational and moral purpose, but rather more basically as providing instructions and examples for how their students and disciples can learn to go about, and live worthwhile and satisfying lives in a world not of their own, or anyone else's, comprehensible purposive making.[7]

To see this point another way, and to cast the Abrahamic religious traditions in even sharper relief, we may consider still other religious traditions. The majority of them, from Central and South to North America, from Africa to Southeast Asia, and everywhere in between, have single creation stories, most of which describe not only creation, but the origins of particular plants, animals, human beings, and other experienced phenomena. But there's a catch: in each instance, certain things are not explained, certain events happen by accident, and/or divinities did what they did because they were in a mood to do so.

The Hawaiian creation poem Kumulipo, for example, begins with the land rising from the ocean. Why there was an ocean is not explained. The ocean is similarly simply a given in the Tokpela, the Hopi narrative of the first world. Contradicting Genesis, the Popol Vuh of the native Guatemalan Mayan peoples describes how the grandmother of all creatures first attempted to create human beings from clay and dirt, but then destroyed her early creations because they were too soft and malleable, and did not make good servants. The second time around she used corn, and was more satisfied with the results.

More familiar to us is Greek mythology. Hesiod tells us what happened at the beginning, but not why, and the same problem plagues the Greeks thereafter: the Delphic Oracle is desperately needed because the gods and goddesses behave capriciously much of the time; their behavior is not reliably predictable. If so wise, why does grey-eyed Athena favor Achilles over Hector, when the latter is far more the decent and likeable of the two? Why does Zeus become so enthralled by Leda that he'll change form in order to seduce her? Why does he punish Prometheus so severely for a benevolent action? Why does Aphrodite cause Helen to fall in love with Paris? Because they felt like it, that's why.

Unlike Judaism, Christianity, and Islam, but of a piece with their Asian kin, none of these religions affirm an intelligible universe capable of being fully understood by human rational and moral faculties. And thus it should not surprise us that the spiritually significant members of these societies—shamans, magicians, healers, witches, sorcerers, gurus, soothsayers, medicine men, priestesses, teachers all—devote their energies to assisting the other members of their societies to get on in this world, to learn how to live *in* it, rather than concentrate on learning *about* it.

Contrast all of this with Genesis 1.1–14, wherein God created the Heavens and the earth, separated them, placed vegetation, animals, and human beings in the latter, all purposefully, and for the good, for reasons which we can all ultimately come to know. Contrast it with Matthew 13.10, wherein Jesus is quoted as saying to the disciples, "To you it has been given to know the secrets of heaven, but to them [i.e., the common people] it has not been given." Contrast it with Sura 21.16 from the Quran, in which Allah says, "We created not the world and all that is in it for our mere amusement"—which is repeated verbatim in Sura 44.

*T*HUS FAR I HAVE FOCUSED ON how different the sacred texts and narratives of the Abrahamic traditions are from other traditions, which is *prima facie* incompatible with my earlier claim that at the most fundamental level, all religious texts and narratives are saying much the same things. The differences, however, especially to those of us steeped in the Abrahamic heritages, must be understood before their far deeper similarities can be equally understood and appreciated. Because we are asked to directly believe the descriptions of the world, and the transcendental world beyond it, as described in the Hebrew scriptures, the New Testament, and the Quran, we quite naturally ask, when we begin the study of other religions, what do their adherents believe about how the universe came to be, is, functions, what is beyond it and what its future holds?

But if my analysis of these other traditions is even roughly on the mark, it follows that this is not the proper way to interrogate or study those other texts and narratives, at least initially. Rather should they be read as providing directions, guiding us to lead more meaningful lives *in this world*, the world of our experience, in which we live and die; they map paths we may follow to aid our embodied selves in enduring suffering and celebrating joy.

The concept of the how and the why of the world being explanatorily intelligible in Judaism, Christianity, and Islam is basic to these three faiths, but it by no means exhausts what they are about. If this be so, then, instead of concentrating solely on how the Abrahamic texts and narratives describe this world and the next, giving us purportedly factual knowledge which we are to believe directly, perhaps we should reread them, focusing on how they, too, may also be providing instruction for us in how to go about in the world; how to live purposively in it, and derive a nonmaterial nurturance therefrom. The basis of such nurturance is religious experience, about which I will speak later in the context of Ludwig Wittgenstein's notion of *das Mystiche*, the mystical.[8] But for now I just want to note that such experiences are seldom had solely on the basis of direct beliefs, from purely cognitive efforts; within specific cultural contexts, equally specific beliefs about how and why this world and the next are constituted as they are may be *sufficient* for having such experiences, but they are not *necessary* therefor; a good many agnostics and others have all had such experiences throughout human history and across cultures.

To elaborate on this point, let me turn for a moment to the nineteenth-century philosopher and theologian Søren Kierkegaard.[9]

In his famous *Either/Or,* and other writings, Kierkegaard maintained that there are three planes on which we may lead our lives; the aesthetic, the ethical, and the religious. In the first of these, we lead our lives unreflectively. The hopes, fears, dreams, nightmares, and aspirations we have are largely due to the influence of our parents, siblings, teachers, friends, and neighbors. What schools we attend are largely determined by parents and peers; what jobs we get are largely determined by what positions are open when we seek one; and what we hope to get from our lives is significantly determined for us by cultural influences.

But almost all of us, according to Kierkegaard, will at some time in our lives have the opportunity to "choose ourselves," a most unusual expression. What

Kierkegaard means by it is that most of us will come to the realization someday that we could have chosen otherwise than the paths we followed. Having come to this painful realization, some of us will accept it, and thereby enter the ethical plane, wherein we assume full responsibility for what we have done, and who we are; we know we must give reasons for what we choose to do, because we are aware, acutely aware, that we could have chosen otherwise.

And adding to the pain is the fact that the ethical life cannot, in the end, sustain us for Kierkegaard. It often obliges us to choose between evil deeds; it can require that we act against the inclinations of true love; we can never do enough ethically, and to say that "I do what I can," is, for him, to engage in self-deception. Faced with this angst, we may sink into despair; a "fear and trembling" can overcome us, and we can become afflicted with a "sickness unto death," to quote the titles of two of his more famous works. What a few of us may do, however, and all of us can do, is confront and admit the absurdity of the descriptive account of this world and the next offered in Christian scripture, straightforwardly admit that this account goes altogether against our rationality, and nevertheless make a "leap of faith"—he is the originator of the expression—that the scriptural account of the world is yet *somehow* true, and we are to live our lives in accordance with that account.

For myself there is much that is beautiful, incisive, and inspiring in Kierkegaard's writings, but there is also something mistaken about his analysis of the human condition, and that something, too common in the whole of Western philosophy and theology, is that the aesthetic, ethical, and spiritual dimensions of our lives are easily distinguishable, and separate spheres of existence. Almost all of the world's religious traditions, especially the Asian, affirm the contrary: that a meaningful human life requires the integration of all three.

But Kierkegaard offers us a special insight into religion by his analysis in that as we progress through his planes of existence, we pass from being relatively unself-conscious on the aesthetic plane, to becoming intensely self-conscious when we enter the ethical— realizing at every step that we alone are responsible for what we have elected to do—and then ascend to being unself-conscious again at a higher level if and when we enter the religious realm. Now I am no longer the sole author of what I do, nor do I wish to be; now I understand fully, and accept, what Jesus said at Gethsemane: "Not as I will, but as thou wilt" (Matthew 26.36).

That Kierkegaard's insight has cross-cultural validity can be seen by examining other sacred texts. "In the calm of self-surrender," Krishna tells Arjuna in the third chapter of the *Bhagavad-Gita*, "you need only rely on me; dream not that you do the warrior's killing, but go forth in battle as you must." The Daoist sage Zhuang Zi says succinctly: "cease (self-) striving; then there will be self-transformation." In a related vein, Confucius admonished his students: "Don't worry about not being acknowledged by others; worry about failing to acknowledge them" (1.16).

I have appealed to Kierkegaard here for a very special reason. To badly paraphrase Kant, I want to delineate what we take to be the scope not only of knowledge, but of belief and faith as well, in order to call attention to a different realm of human experience.

What all of the imperatives just proffered share, and have in common with the imperatives of yet other traditions, is the necessity of engaging in a discipline of ego-reduction, a move away from I—the experiencer— to what is actually being experienced. Surely the knowledge gained in the Garden of Eden by partaking of the forbidden fruit is that we are mortal, and that one day we will indeed return to become again the ashes and dust whence we have come. With such knowledge it becomes more difficult to stand in awe of a sunrise, delight in a bird's song, celebrate our children's first hesitant footsteps, or become wholly immersed in sharing food, drink, and conversation with those we hold dear, for it will come to us, sooner, later, implicitly or explicitly, subtly or forcefully, but always surely, that one day we will not be here to stand in awe, or delight, or celebrate, or be immersed in these earthly activities. And our current appreciation of participating in these activities can all too easily be diminished thereby, for in our heart of hearts we all do know that someday we will die, and be dead forever. And the more ego-filled we are, the more easily these thoughts can diminish the quality of our everyday life.

I do not believe philosophical and theological—that is, purely cognitive—efforts to come directly to terms with this knowledge will be effective for most people, and being told to simply have faith in the literal truth of scripture will fall on increasingly deaf ears in the twenty-first century. Organ transplants are of course with us now, and perhaps cloning techniques and/or genetic implants can increase our life span, and it is even conceivable that there might someday be a magic pill to arrest the ravages of aging so that we all might live to be 175 years old or more. So what? This merely postpones the problem. Here I am reminded of a *New Yorker* cartoon in which two elderly gentlemen replete with wings and harps are sitting on a cloud, with one saying to the other: "I'm not sure I'd have wanted to live to age 83 if I had realized I'd be 83 forever."

Relatedly, it is becoming increasingly difficult for sensitive and intelligent people to continue to be comforted by being assured that they will come to apprehend the purpose and reason for their embodied existence in some vaguely-defined hereafter. Consider Paul's memorable words in First Corinthians (13.8):

Now I see in a mirror dimly; but then face to face. Now I know in part, then I will understand fully, as I have been understood fully.

Note first that here we have yet another affirmation that everything is ultimately explanatorily intelligible; as a justification for continuing to question what, how, and why, astrophysicists and biologists could ask for no more.

But as time goes on, intelligent people will not, I think, be sustained by Paul's words taken literally, for intelligence will generate nagging questions: Why can't our Creator explain why He created us while we are still embodied, enabling us to live more tranquil and useful human lives? Why would an all-benevolent deity deign to create such brief and often agonizing placement examinations here merely to determine our eternal transcendental status elsewhere?

I do not believe answers to such questions can be forthcoming on the basis of standard religious beliefs regarding scripture, or a Kierkegaardian leap of faith that somehow they are literally true, for both require us to divest ourselves entirely of our rational cognitive capacities. Being unwilling to renounce the science I have been taught, or to renounce the discipline of philosophy in which I have been trained professionally, and respectful of the principles of pure logic which must govern all human thought and communication, I must, if I am to insist on the importance of the study of sacred texts and narratives, suggest that we seek in them different kinds of knowledge and belief, generating different patterns of faith.

IN THE FIRST PLACE, each of our lives may be said to be a story. But every story, in order to be even minimally interesting and worthy of contemplation and/or emulation, must have a beginning, a development, and an end. Lacking any of these elements there would be no story, and especially without an end, there would be no closure, hence no whole to be encompassed, reflected upon, imitated, or passed on to succeeding generations. We can only applaud the heroes or heroines of a tale who narrowly avoid death while struggling for the good in the knowledge that one day, eventually full of years, they will indeed pass to their reward; if we believed they might live forever, what would there be to commend, or to applaud? The Olympian gods and goddesses may have many virtues in addition to their vices, but courage is not among them; only mortals can be truly courageous.

The moral of this argument is as easy to understand cognitively as it is difficult to implement psychically: we must come to confront directly and accept our mortality, and then go on to live a productive and satisfying life undisturbed by morbid thoughts of the transitory nature of our existence. Easier said than done. Good luck.[10]

Yet the Abrahamic traditions no less than others tell us how to go about doing this, how to become less ego-filled, more unself-conscious, and thereby more open to the full panoply of human experiences, including religious experiences. The latter are often momentary, but their effects linger. With some, the experience can go on for hours, even days perhaps. And for a very few, it is enduring.[11] In the whole of religious literature, and in most of the accounts of religious experience proffered in the social sciences— wherein too many researchers have tended to eat the menu instead of the dinner—such experiences are labeled "mystical," which has come to be synonymous with the ineffable, the obscure, and/or the inexplicable.[12] I will elaborate on the nature of religious experiences in a moment, but let me first briefly outline several specific paths every religious tradition proffers to its followers for having such experiences. They all suggest, separately and together, a number of ways of becoming less self-conscious, less "I" absorbed, and more open to the experience of being in the world, of being in a place, of being with others, of living more fully in the present.

Virtually no sacred texts, to my knowledge, offer only a single path, a single spiritual discipline, in order to experience the sacred *in the secular*;[13] not there, but *here* and *now*. On the contrary, sacred texts and narratives outline a multiplicity of paths leading to spiritual experiences (which is why a facile reading of those texts might suggest that they are saying contradictory things at times). But closer reading suggests that those texts are saying different things to different people within their own tradition, offering several ways for following a spiritual path to those who wish to tread one.

The most common path is simply acceptance of the overall world view presented in the texts of a religious tradition, and acceptance thereby of the necessity of submitting—becoming less individualistic, less ego-full—to the sacrifices prescribed in those texts, adherence to the rituals thereof, attendance to prayer, the observance of holy days, and more. Jesus was not the first religious thinker to realize that the mere formalistic practices dictated by a tradition could be utterly devoid of spiritual significance, but for many people, in each tradition, full participation in these prescribed practices has proven efficacious; these practices can be a path to the sacred by faith, by submitting to the demands that faith makes on its followers through the sacred texts, and through their symbols, rituals, and traditions.

A second path, especially among the intelligentsia in each tradition, is through scholarship. This method of ego-reduction obliges an absorption in the sacred texts themselves: writing commentaries and glosses on them, retranslating them, becoming a cleric perhaps, all in the attempt to enable the author or authors of the original texts to continue to speak meaningfully to later audiences. Here the Talmudic and Confucian traditions are especially strong, but every tradition has its scholars—that is, those who write *scholia*—who discipline themselves to be faithful and true to their texts.

A third path to spiritual experience is through good works, leading an exemplary moral life. For Hindus and Buddhists this is the path of *karma-yog;* for the early Confucians it is the major path to sagehood,[14] but is a common theme in all other religious traditions as well, which uniformly offer salvation or liberation to the unselfish who eschew personal and material well-being in favor of good works, struggling actively to overcome pain and suffering, and/or to promote justice, freedom, and equality.

Still another religious path is the meditative, or contemplative. The followers of this path undertake, in a variety of means, a rigorously prescribed physical and mental discipline in order to achieve a religious experience directly or indirectly, but usually immediate (the "mystical" experience). Those who have such experiences uniformly lament the inability of ordinary language to describe this extraordinary event, which is no less uniformly described as being "beyond the senses." (Beatific visions and voices may well be genuine religious experiences as well, but "mystical" they are not.)[15]

These are four paths, four spiritual disciplines, every sacred text with which I am familiar provides guidelines to follow, which I label the (1) faith, (2) scholarly, (3) moral, and (4) contemplative paths respectively.

There are, of course, other paths. It is well known that in Chinese and Japanese Buddhism, for example, training in the tea ceremony, martial arts,[16] and landscape architecture can also serve as spiritual disciplines, as do the apprenticeships served by shamans and shamanesses the world over. And it may not be too much of a stretch to say that even the Christian-inspired scientific tradition in the West can be seen, by some at least, as a spiritual discipline: the struggle to achieve objectivity surely requires rigorous efforts at ego-reduction.

There are still other paths, I believe, especially one which requires a keen sensitivity to and absorption in the natural world which sustains us, but I will not dwell thereon now, because such works as *Walden*, *A Sand County Almanac*, *Pilgrim at Tinker Creek*, and *The Dream of the Earth* are not yet fully accepted as sacred texts.[17]

And because my focus herein is on how everyone may profit by rethinking what sacred texts and narratives might be saying to us, I will not take up yet another possible path, namely, foregoing the workaday world by entering a monastery or convent within a particular tradition, except to note that those who elect this path will be obliged to follow, with varying degrees of emphasis, all of the first four specific paths just adumbrated.

It must also be noted that not all religious traditions place equal emphasis on all of these paths.

The contemplative path is accorded great weight in Hinduism and Buddhism, less so in Christianity, despite the lives and works of Meister Eckhart, San Juan de la Cruz, and many others. The Christian tradition also no longer accords its scholars the same respect and veneration accorded the scholars of other traditions. Classical Daoism says little about either the faith or scholarly paths.[18] Islam acknowledges its Sufis, but celebrates its religious scholars, and champions the faithful, as does Judaism, with both Kabbalists and Rabbis as well as the Orthodox. But all traditions describe all paths to follow, and each has its exemplars thereof.

Catholics, for example, may simply keep the faith; or they can find inspiration in the life and writings of the scholar/philosopher/theologians Gabriel Marcel or Evelyn Underhill; or they can emulate Dorothy Day and Daniel Berrigan in struggling for peace and justice, or follow the example of the Trappist contemplative Thomas Merton.[19]

This multiplicity of voices with which all religious traditions speak is as it should be. Most people are obliged to work long and hard to sustain themselves and their families. They have no time to become scholars or contemplatives. Moral they must be, and giving to the best of their abilities, but it is the faith path most of them must follow as a spiritual discipline. Modern scholars are more inclined to sit in chairs rather than in the lotus position, and meditators are not infrequently iconoclastic with respect to their texts and traditions. All, however, are told to follow at least to some extent the moral path, to which I call attention because it implies that every religious tradition has manifold scriptural resources with which to challenge and condemn the more fanatical and violent of its adherents; moral imperialism, especially of a Western philosophical sort, need not rear its ugly head here.

Another reason for calling especial attention to the ethical path insisted upon in all traditions is that it provides a partial answer to the question of how to live an integrated life– the importance of which is insisted upon in almost all traditions—in a disintegrating society. This topic is a large one, too large to consider herein: suffice it to say that I believe a number of societies are disintegrating today (which is a major reason for fundamentalist/fanatical movements) and deep moral commitment will be necessary to arrest and reverse the disintegration through fundamental socioeconomic and political change, and religious renewal.

Now, FINALLY, I MUST ADDRESS DIRECTLY the nature of the specific kind of spiritual experiences that are my concern in this lecture, a promissory note I owe you, and without which my prior arguments and reflections will probably be of little moment. Some contemporary scholars of religion question whether the concept of "religious experience" can be made meaningful,[20] and many more wish to distinguish between religious experience and mystical experiences. Herein I must bracket the skeptical thrust of the former claim, and remain silent on the nature of a purely *mystical* experience. What I want to do is define religious experience as Wittgenstein suggested for *das Mystiche*, namely, as the sense that we are absolutely safe.[21]

This is a most incisive and original description, but is still somewhat enigmatic, and has a decidedly Christian flavor: we are "secure in God's hands." My work with Confucian texts suggests more generally a sense of belonging, fully belonging, in their case to those who have preceded us, those in whose midst we live, and those who will follow us. In the Abrahamic faiths, it is a feeling of atonement, or, as I would prefer to syllabically resegment the term, at-one-ment. "Attunement" is also appropriate.

As argued above, each of the world's religious traditions offers us several ways, several paths we might follow in order to achieve this sense of belonging, of safety, of at-one-ment, or attunement. And we may directly believe that these paths are efficacious because the history of each tradition provides irrefutable evidence that countless numbers of each tradition's adherents have had such experiences; with or without much metaphysics, or factual knowledge of the world, they have achieved the wisdom of how to live fully in it with grace, dignity, and contentment.

Thus I submit that it is fully rational to indirectly believe, have faith, that there is much truth in the sacred texts and narratives of the world's religions, even though much that is said therein cannot be believed literally as factual accounts of this or any other world. In the same way, because the equations developed by Oppenheimer and his colleagues work— most of the time, anyway—so too we should indirectly believe, have faith, that there is truth in his remarks quoted earlier, even though they are logically contradictory if taken literally as factual accounts of this or any other world.

This sense of belonging, of safety, can take several forms. We can come to a feeling of being at one first and foremost with the human race, and secondarily with nature (Confucianism), or the reverse emphasis (classical Daoism, many Native American and African religions), or with one's own depths in relation to all else (Buddhism), or with something transcendental (Hinduism, the Abrahamic religions); the forms vary from tradition to tradition, and at times even within the same tradition. But however different their focus, and how they describe reality, all of the world's religions provide us in common with several disciplinary paths for learning how to get on in the world, enabling us to have that experience of belonging, of safety, of at-one-ment, of attunement—in *this* world, *here* and *now*.

The importance of a sense of belonging as an important condition for human well-being is illustrated, I believe, by a perverse form of generating that sense, cult membership. Ecstasy, union, a willingness to die, and much else put forward by charismatic leaders are all made possible by the strong sense of belonging to the cult. I am not at all a scholar of religious cults, and am fully aware of how a sensationalist media can distort their beliefs and activities, but it does seem to me that the members thereof are more prone to frenzy than serenity, more self-absorbed than morally committed, and their sense of belonging stems from an exclusionary rather than inclusionary orientation: only the few will be saved, the others will not. Equally significant, cults do not appear to belong to a place, nor to emphasize the discipline of feeling a kinship with the nonhuman world.[22]

To more fully describe this inclusionary religious experience is difficult. It is certainly not some form of extrasensory perception, but rather an additive to our sensory experiences. As a simple illustration, imagine returning to your *alma mater* with some friends who have not been there before. As you walk the campus together, you will all see, hear, and smell the same things, but experience them differently. Your friends will have directly all of the visual, aural, and olfactory sensations that you do, but in addition, you will have a sense of belonging there, and they will not. And I would suggest that such experiences have a strong aesthetic, as well as a spiritual dimension to them.

This sense is a feeling of being a part of, at one with, something larger than ourselves, something that was present before we came to be, something to which we contribute now, and something which will endure after us. The world's religions affirm that this sense of belonging, of safety, of at-one-ment or attunement may be experienced by everyone, and they all provide disciplines by means of which we may become less ego-full, and hence more open to such experiences. The texts offer no guarantees that we will have these experiences; this is ultimately a gift of the spirit. But they do affirm that such experiences may come to us if the spirit can get the ego sufficiently out of the way.

For all these reasons, I commend the sacred texts and narratives of the world's religions to your careful attention and study. Reread, and read in conjunction with the texts of other traditions, each tradition can be renewed, and come to be seen as collaborative rather than competitive with the others, and thereby, as conducive to lessening the distance between "us" and "them."

Perhaps by seriously attempting to plumb the spiritual depths of *other* traditions we can come to more deeply understand and appreciate our own—an effort that might well provide rewarding even to those who do not feel as if they are a part of any religious tradition. These studies must be undertaken with great care, with sympathy, and with the fully rational belief and faith that all of these texts contain much truth, the discernment of which can aid us in living more meaningful and satisfying lives. Such studies cannot by themselves insure that we will find our way in the twenty-first century, but they will reduce significantly, I believe, our chances of becoming irretrievably lost in it.

Commentary by
Huston Smith

IT IS A VERY GREAT HONOR, and speaking even more personally, a very great happiness for me to be able to share this evening (in unequal proportions I'm very glad to say) with my dear friend Henry Rosemont. I'm very mindful that the announcement for this occasion said very clearly that my response was to be brief, and therefore I shall forego a more elaborate response. "Brief" is a very wise word, as I could easily turn this into a nostalgia trip and tell you about our lunches in Cambridge where it was Henry and I against the other philosophers in the Bermuda Triangle of Harvard, Princeton, and Cornell who said there was no philosophy outside of the Western world. I could tell you about those lunches. I could tell you about being at his own institution several times, especially on the occasion when he was awarded St. Mary's College's first endowed chair; but enough of reverie.

We've had a very great and rich paper. What I will do is to first distill what I take to be the essence of Henry's message to us this evening, because if I'm wrong there, well then, what follows will be off the mark. I will then close by raising two questions for him.

He wants, and I'm sure that we're all with him, to validate the great enduring wisdom traditions of the world's religions, and to insist that they have not outlived their usefulness. Their usefulness is personal, helping us still with directives for living meaningful lives, but also social, in their potential for creating a more just and more peaceful world. However, Henry goes on from that premise to say that we need to revision them, and the key to this revisioning is to distinguish between "direct" and "indirect" ways of reading sacred texts. By direct, I take it he means literal, and also pretty much what they say about the world. Those fall into the camp of the direct reading. He is proposing, moreover, that because those have lost their credibility, we move to an indirect reading. And there he makes an initial distinction between the Abrahamic traditions in the West, and the traditions in South Asia and East Asia.

In the Abrahamic tradition, an indirect reading shows that they tell us, in part, that we have a rational, intelligible world. That deliverance has led on into modern science, which has occurred in the West only, and not originally in the other traditions. Indirect readings of Indian, Chinese, and other sacred texts has to do, I take it, with moral and spiritual directives as to how we can live productive, satisfying, meaningful, and contributing lives. Starting with the West and having then made this detour to India and China, he proposes that we bring that same indirect reading into the Abrahamic religions, and look to them primarily for similar directives.

Henry, I am your student here, and if I got it wrong, you will have an opportunity to tell me. But that, I take it, is the basic structure of the lecture.

Now I want to proceed to two questions. I was looking for, but did not find in the paper, with one exception, any mention of the word "metaphysics," or perhaps even "cosmology." I want to propose that this is the way I think of it: cosmology has to do with the nature, the furniture of this physical universe and how it works. And I agree that the traditional sects have been retired on the issue of cosmology. But there remains a matter of metaphysics, Henry. Unless you have bought into the postmodern deconstruction of metaphysics, either in its early version of saying "it's all meaningless," or in the later versions where—unless you buy into one of those, what status would you give to the metaphysical dimensions of these texts? I remind you I am not speaking about this physical world externally, but to the possibility of other dimensions of reality. Let me just take a quick tour around the world.

In China, (although I am very reluctant to say anything about China in Henry's presence), we have earth, but then we also have Heaven. There is one dictum by Confucius, "Of Heaven and earth, only Heaven is great." Now does that have any metaphysical meaning? When we turn to Daoism, we do have the Dao of nature, but we also have the Dao that is "unspoken." We all remember that wonderful quote in the forty-second chapter of the *Dao De Jing*: "There is a being—wonderful, perfect— how quiet it is, how giving it is . . . I do not know its name, so I call it the Dao, and I rejoice in its Way."

What are we to make of a text like this? Does it simply translate into moral directives for leading a meaningful life? Or, does it point to something that has ontological reality? And, very quickly, what are we to make of *sunyata*? Of *nirvana* as contrasted with *samsara* in India? And in the Western tradition, what are we to make of "that in whose image" (rational as you point out) "we are"? Are these all to be moralized and translated into directives for leading a meaningful and constructive life in this world? Or, do they suggest that there may be regions of reality that slip through the nets of science? To lay my cards on the table, I happen to suspect—more than suspect, I happen to believe—that they do alert modern scientistic society to its blindness, calling our attention to domains of existence which the West has pretty much forgotten. Of course, in the Western philosophical tradition, to conclude my quick tour, I should assuredly mention that paradigm of the allegory of Plato's cave and the sun that lies outside it.

My second question relates to it. I really liked what you moved up to in the notion of the mystical, absolute safety, and the notion of belonging. But again, are these simply psychological states that these traditions give us as directives for how we can come to these feelings? Or, do they dig deeper into the nature of things to describe a reality, the ultimate reality which gives grounds for us to think that we are not just making it up when we have these sentiments of safety and belonging?

These, then, are two issues I would hope you could take up to conclude a wonderful lecture.

Response and Discussion

HR: As he so frequently does, Huston gets
right to the heart of matters when he challenges my
silence on metaphysical issues taken up in sacred
texts. I am pleased that he agrees with me that the
cosmologies described in these texts can no longer be
credited as describing the world of human experience,
but that still leaves open the possibility of their
being "other dimensions of reality," or "domains of
existence," as he puts it, that "slip through the nets
of science."

This is a most important issue, but my silence on
it was intentional, for a number of reasons. First,
these "other dimensions of reality" have traditionally
been taken as belonging to a *transcendental* realm,
usually defined as one on which our physical and
human worlds depend wholly for their existence, but
which is not in any way dependent on them; a world
"wholly other" than the one we live in. Such a
transcendental "world" is suggested in some Indian
philosophical works, but is otherwise, in my view,
characteristic of only the Abrahamic traditions of the
West. No such metaphysical claims invest Buddhist,
Confucian, or Daoist texts as I read them, and
while these latter religions, and all others, have
supernatural entities described in their oral or written
canons, these entities remain altogether linked to *this*
world. The *tian* (misleadingly translated as "Heaven")
of the Confucians, and the Daoist *dao* both have
religious connotations, but they do not refer to a
realm conceptually separate from the world of human

experience and effort.[23] The many gods and goddesses described and venerated in the Chinese tradition all share the quality of being deceased human beings, ancestors or otherwise.

A second reason for my silence on metaphysical matters concerns language. If, as I have argued, a more serious effort to obtain interfaith understanding is to take place, a keen sensitivity to the nuances of language and language use will be necessary, not only with respect to our own native tongue, but as well to the many other languages employed to articulate religious experience. I endorse fully the Chomskyan claim—initially counterintuitive—that human beings basically speak one language, with (not inconsequential) dialectical variations; thus I must reject the Sapir-Whorf hypothesis of linguistic determinisim *cum* relativity.[24] But these dialectical variations—in their phonological, syntactic, and pragmatic dimensions no less than the semantic— certainly *influence* the way(s) we think about and describe reality, and consequently statements which rely on specific metaphysical assumptions or presuppositions for their plausibility should be approached with great caution in cross-cultural interfaith dialogues.

In other work I have taken up the importance of attending in new ways to issues of translation and interpretation when engaged in comparative philosophical and religious research, and in interfaith dialogue.[25] The linguistic issues are too complex to

RESPONSE AND DISCUSSION

rehearse now, but I can hint at some of what I mean by noting that no one attempts to translate terms such as *karma* or *dharma*; they are simply included now in the English lexicon. *Dao* is slowly achieving this status, and as Roger Ames and I argued in our new translation of the *Analects, tian* too should be glossed and transliterated, for "Heaven" is too fraught with Judaic-Christian cosmological and theological concepts to serve as translation for *tian*.[26]

Still another reason for my silence on metaphysical matters is that I do not need to raise them in order to argue for the ongoing relevance and importance of the world's religions for the citizens of the twenty-first century. The major thrust of my remarks, however inadequately proffered, has been that even the most dyed-in-the-wool, empirically and logically oriented agnostic rationalist has good reasons for attending to the sacred texts of the world's religions with great respect, in the fully rational belief that those texts can aid us measurably in leading productive and ultimately satisfying lives, enhancing the joys thereof, and mitigating their sorrows.

This is a woefully brief response to your incisive questions, Huston, but I hope that they will at least convey the general direction in which I am going. Perhaps some further amplification will occur as I attempt to respond to audience questions; many hands are going up, and I would like to recognize other challenges, comments, and inquiries.

QUESTION: I quite agree that there is something formally similar among all religions, namely the sense of security, this sense of belonging. But how can we dialogue based on this sense of security which we all share, as you argue, if we divorce that sense of security from the metaphysics that nurtures it in the different traditions? Or from the positions against metaphysics, for example, in some Buddhist traditions? We might have these formal similarities among all the traditions, but if we take out the content, what basis do we have for dialogue? For example, how could a Christian sense of safety and belonging based on Trinity, be in dialogue with the Buddhist sense, based on *sunyata*, or emptiness?

HR: That's a splendid question. Let me first respond by throwing one of its implications back at you. If two traditions have incompatible metaphysics, then the possibility of a genuine dialogue and understanding between them is almost surely not going to happen. You will end up only with debate. But if we start out on a lower, nonmetaphysical level, we can come to appreciate that the view of the world a Buddhist has somehow helps Buddhists come to terms with their human lives in the same way a Christian view helps Christians. This is a substantive similarity, I believe, not simply a formal one.[27] And with that beginning, we can hope that Buddhists, as well as

Hindus, Muslims, and so on, can come to see how beliefs, and attendant symbols and practices, can contribute to the meaningfulness of human lives in differing religious traditions, and therefore come to have a sympathy for those ways of looking at the world, if not an acceptance of them. A quick example. Statues of the Indian skull-necklaced goddess Kali may well be horrifying to Christians, even if viewed less hysterically than in the film *Indiana Jones and the Temple of Doom*. But clearly a crucifix, especially a bleeding one, can be no less repellent to a Hindu, no matter how much it signals the sacred to a Catholic. For a naive Buddhist the sacrament of communion may well smack of ritual cannibalism even though that is not at all the way Episcopalians interpret the ceremony, although the latter, might, with equal naiveté, be tempted to dismiss Buddhist *sunyata* merely as a form of nihilism.[28]

Again, I would insist that the basic question we must keep before us in studying religions is how rational, sensitive, and moral human beings can adhere to spiritual traditions very different from those with which we are familiar, especially with respect to their metaphors and symbols.[29] If this question is kept initially uppermost, we might then go on to come to a fuller appreciation of the *moral* dimensions of religious traditions, and thus come to see how all of them, as I hinted briefly in my lecture, have manifold resources to generate more universally acceptable ideals of justice and equality, with attendant renunciations of violence as a means for realizing those ideals.

That is, when you start taking the sacred texts seriously and see how much is in them that you can appreciate and sympathize with spiritually, the ethical will follow, I think, (as will the aesthetic) and much of the sting of the charge of cultural imperialism on the part of the West goes away. Part of the sting will remain, however, because we will come to see as we more deeply appreciate those other moral traditions that the Western heritage doesn't have a monopoly either on moral virtue, spiritual insight, or aesthetic sensitivity.

This is necessary if we are to have both a greater cross-cultural dialogue on how to live in a more peaceful and just world, and how each of us, each tradition, might contribute to helping the others to genuinely live an authentic, integrated life aesthetically, ethically, and spiritually. That's a sketchy beginning toward an answer to a splendid question.

QUESTION: As the problems of the twenty-first century push us toward hopelessness and apathy, are the world's religions becoming any more or less relevant in combating that hopelessness and apathy?

HR: They are becoming more relevant, I believe. If unjust and immoral actions are taking place, moral agents in every culture will struggle to stop those actions by the best means at their disposal. You struggle in order to stop those actions. But if your efforts are not successful, after a time you may well get discouraged, or feel that change cannot occur, and become apathetic; this will almost surely happen to everyone who struggles only to bring about the changes, that is, those who are struggling to win the battle, and is one of the untoward consequences of a purely utilitarian or pragmatic moral orientation.

But we can also struggle against the evils of the world simply because they are evils, full stop; so long as they endure, the struggle must go on, witness must be borne. This way of thinking is far more characteristic of religious ethics, I believe, than secular moral theories, and the importance of the difference between them can make a difference.

As is often the case, Confucius can serve as a model here. When traveling from state to state, one or two disciples preceded the retinue in order to secure lodging in the next town. In one instance, the disciple Zilu approached a town, and the gatekeeper asked him "Who is your master?" Zilu replied, "Master Kong of Lu." The gatekeeper interrogated him further: "Isn't he the one who knows it's no use, but keeps trying?" "That's him," answered Zilu (14.38, amended).

QUESTION: Our society is overbalanced with a view toward the rational, and subsequently towards self-centeredness. The result is overconsumption, lack of regard for the individual's effects on the community. How can an Eastern religious perspective assist with balancing this perspective, in other words to get rid of greed and enhance the view of the whole?

HR: Part of the answer is that reading the non-Western texts will help you read the texts of the Abrahamic traditions in a different way as well. Attending carefully to the nonmaterialist thrust of most of the world's religions can remind us that it is very hard to quote scripture in favor of the televangelists, in favor of this overconsumption, in favor of all the things that are destructive of community, and contribute to a meaninglessness that is increasingly affecting all of our lives. It is very hard to quote from the Gospels, the Hebrew scriptures, or the Quran to justify the present "American way of life." "Not by bread alone," is fairly central. It is true that God helps those who help themselves, but we must love our neighbor as ourselves. "May the best man win" is more than offset by many examples of the view that "It is not whether you win or lose, but how you play the game that counts." The English jurist Coke said that "Every man's home is his castle," yet we agree with the English cleric John Donne that "No man is an island." We have the resources within the Western tradition to combat rampant materialism and the destruction of our social and natural environments.[30] Many of those resources have been given short shrift since the rise of capitalism, but they are there, to be interpreted anew against the background of examining other traditions, and incorporating their wisdom accordingly. And, of course, the same may be said for the other traditions as well.

QUESTION: Regarding security, which also includes a sense of belonging that you mentioned, Annie Dillard said, "We are most deeply asleep at the switches when we fancy we have any control at all." Isn't the idea of religion precisely to help us understand that there is no such thing as "security?"

HR: I had hoped to get a few easy questions; that's another hard but equally excellent one. Dillard is, of course, working with the sense of security that comes from a fairly literal reading of the Abrahamic texts wherein we are told, again, that we are "secure in God's hands," which, when we observe and contemplate nature as deeply as she does, seems assuredly not to be the case. Such observation and contemplation renders highly implausible Leibnizian and other arguments that all is for the best in this best of all possible worlds, and a part of what Dillard is doing, I believe, is updating Voltaire's critique of such arguments.

It is interesting to note that Dillard's questioning of simplistic faith in God here applies equally to simplistic faith in science to make us more secure by the "conquest of nature"—again, a concept unique to the Abrahamic traditions, and stemming from the faith as well that the universe is explanatorily intelligible. And for those who defend the faith in science to give us security on the grounds of the progress that has been made in this regard, I would reply that this entails an unusual definition of the word "progress": our ability to arrest death has been more than matched by our ability to spread it, and the percentage of human beings who go to bed hungry every night—if they have a bed—is surely higher than it was three or more centuries ago, everywhere in the world.

This is not a plea to return to feudalism, or the Stone Age. Your quote from Dillard is in the context of an analogy she draws between the incredible complexity of chaotic interactions in nature with a railroad system that has grown, unmanaged, to the point where its workings are uncontrollable, with trains crashing everywhere.[31] But let's think of her analogy in a different way. Railroads are a human, not a natural, creation. There are problems inherent with them, but if managed with an eye to people and not profits, railroads can move those who need to go somewhere else with a means of doing so that is far more humanly interactive, efficient, aesthetically pleasing, energy saving, and earth sustaining than SUVs by the millions barreling along millions of acres of asphalt and concrete, with drivers comforted only by cell phones and guns in the glove box, attempting to avoid the large trailer-trucks that move material goods–freight–in a manner far more inefficient and ecologically unsound than trains can move those goods.

Relatedly on security: a basic element of security is food security, which the rich of the world but not the poor enjoy: this type of security also bears on the issue of fundamentalism and fanaticism in religious traditions. The middle classes and ruling elites in these traditions overwhelmingly do not resort to violence in advancing their beliefs; only the mind-numbingly and bone-weary poor do this, which is not merely a coincidence. Although some would have it so, the distinction is not to be drawn between the educated and the noneducated, for it is difficult to receive an education if there are no schools within fifty miles of your home, and even if there are, it is difficult to attend to your studies when you haven't eaten in three days.

But like railroads, the economic distribution of food is a human creation, and hence controllable; if it can be done, as it is at present, altogether unjustly, then it can be done justly too. Food is essential for life, and consequently should not, perhaps, be seen as a commodity on a par with VCRs, automobiles, electric toothbrushes, and cigarette lighters; perhaps societies ought not to be measured, as economists and some other social scientists are wont to do, by how much food they produce, but rather by how equitably they distribute their produce. If such be done, I would suggest that both the quality and quantity of violence in the world would decrease significantly, religiously or otherwise inspired;

occasionally, but seldom, do people with a secure food supply wish to wreak havoc on their neighbors.

A final point on Dillard. I would maintain that although she does indeed convey, movingly, the sense of the uncontrollability of nature to which you rightfully call attention, she nevertheless has a strong sense of belonging at her cabin and environs at Tinker Creek, which is one reason I mentioned her work in the lecture. In many passages her full absorption in what she is perceiving is obvious, even when what she is perceiving is fairly gory. She is fully absorbed, has an affinity and affection for, a sense of belonging in her little world that far surpasses her feelings of helplessness and/or estrangement. At least that is the way I read her.[32]

QUESTION: The word itself—"metaphysics"— would suggest "beyond the physical," the presupposition of something beyond. Isn't this an oxymoron, attempting to describe the metaphysical with the physical?

HR: Another excellent question, to which I would love to hear Huston's response. My own must be in stages, and hinge crucially on my perhaps idiosyncratic reading of the Western philosophical tradition as inherited from the ancient Greeks.

We all know that the term "metaphysics" itself derives from an arbitrary decision on the part of his editors to arrange the works of Aristotle in a certain way. But in his works, no less than Thales and Heraclitus ("all is water," "all is fire"), physicality, the "stuff" of *this* world, is never lost; there is nothing transcendental in these claims. Greek ontologies were challenged, of course, by later metaphysicians: Descartes claimed two substances, Spinoza one, and Leibniz an indefinitely large number of them. But all of these modern thinkers, and many others, would describe themselves today, I think, as doing science; were they to be reincarnated today, they would seek appointments in mathematics, biology, or physics departments, not philosophy, for they were endeavoring to provide the foundational elements for the scientific discoveries of their day. Of course, Leibniz wrote the *Natural Theology of the Chinese* and the *Theodicy*, as well as the *Monadology*; but he wrote the latter for very different reasons than he wrote the former, both of which metaphysically require a Christian transcendental realm in a way the *Monadology* does not.[33]

There are (at least) two seemingly telling counterexamples to this claim about the Greek intellectual heritage, the first being Plato's Forms, or Ideas (*eidos*), and the other, Socrates's autobiographical remarks in the *Apology* about abandoning what we would today refer to as the "scientific method" as a way of obtaining knowledge.

But I read these examples as attempts to come to grips with discoveries in geometry made by Pythagorean thinkers who preceded them, in days far precedent to the works of Leibniz and Newton on the calculus.

We all know, or at least believe, that if a statement is true, it must refer to, be about, something that is the case, which we can verify by observation. We also know, or at least believe, that any diagonal that we actually draw connecting the end points of a right triangle with both sides equal as one, will have a finite length. Unfortunately the Pythagorean Theorem shows conclusively that this is not true: √2—to which the Greeks would not give a symbol as a number—is a nonterminating decimal fraction; and a related argument holds for circles and π. Both Socrates and Plato opted for geometry over observation, and endeavored to justify their option; but this is a long way both from modern science and from the transcendental world of Judaism and Christianity, Augustine notwithstanding. "What is truly real?" is not a question asked in the philosophical and religious traditions of most cultures—and India is only a partial exception—but it is a straightforward one to ask when mathematical developments precede the formative periods of philosophical and religious speculation historically.[34]

In sum—and harking back to linguistic sensitivities mentioned earlier—even if I could somehow translate "What is truly real?" into the classical Chinese language of Confucius, I would suspect he would be no less perplexed by it than if asked, in response to his "rectification of names" arguments, to comment on the linguistic significance of the famous "colorless green ideas sleep furiously."[35]

What I conclude from these reflections is that if "metaphysics" is defined only narrowly, then only thinkers in the West have engaged in it. I am deeply suspicious of such a claim and its chauvinistic overtones, and believe a more open definition is needed for genuine interfaith dialogues and comparative philosophical research to go forward.

QUESTION: The central message of your thesis has something to do with the idea that the power and most valuable message of all the world's religions has to do with what you call "ego-reduction," or "ego-shrinkage." And yet, the most central value in the world today, in both the United States and China, is ego-expansion, selfishness, and so forth. What does that mean, then, for the world's religions? What role are they to take? Are they to become more iconoclastic in going against the prevailing grain? How can they seriously be heard by populations that are moving more and more towards ego-enlargement and self-gratification? What stance do they assume, whether in Asia or America, Eastern or Western?

HR: I most definitely think that the basic truths contained in the sacred texts of the world's religions "go against the grain" of the poisonous ethos of contemporary self-centered materialism, wherein flesh and blood human beings play no role, leaving only those with money—that is, potential purchasers/consumers—acknowledged as existent by the advertising-driven propaganda machine also known as the U.S. media. Given that an increasingly destructive capitalism is not only dominating our lives, but our ways of thinking about our lives as well, I personally believe that purely secular alternatives thereto will not gain much purchase; rather must we look, at least in part, to the traditions of the sacred, East and West, for the revisioning and renewal of our lives.[36]

As I hoped to make clear in my lecture, I do not see the distinction between the secular and the sacred as an ontological one. A transcendental realm there may well be, but by focusing on it as developed in the West we have not only failed to understand and appreciate fully other religious traditions, we have lost sight of much of our own as well. As numerous Indian sages have instructed us, advanced spiritual understanding eventuates in appreciating that *nirvana* and *samsara* are not disparate, but rather that the former is deeply imbedded in the latter. And although there are no close lexical analogues for either "secular" or "sacred" in the Chinese texts, those texts are also best understood, I believe, by appreciating how the Chinese sages are telling us how to more fully dwell in the secular to make it sacred.

These instructions from our friends from the East clearly lead to the ego-reduction of which we have spoken, but let me come at the problem from another philosophical direction, one more central to the Western intellectual heritage.

Huston, in his remarks, suggested that my lack of ontological commitment to "other domains of reality" left me with only the "merely psychological" to defend my claim for the importance of the world's religions in the twenty-first century. Although I disagree with Huston only with great reluctance on any issue, there is, I regret, a difference between us here which I hope the following remarks might bridge, at least in part.

The rapture we feel hearing a piece of beautiful music played superbly; sharing the joy of a friend after some accomplishment; grief felt at the loss of a loved one; all of these and a great many others may be called psychological states, but calling them "mere" can cause us to lose sight of the fact that they are the basic stuff of our lives. They appear to be universal states, found in all cultures past and present, and if I have not been radically wrong in my account of religious experiences, these too, appear to be "psychological states" found in all cultures. But because they serve to enhance and enrich our other experiences, I want to give them the human importance I believe they deserve, which was the major focus of my lecture and which can all too easily be neglected or disparaged by engaging in too much metaphysics and theology—or psychology.

Relatedly, Huston suggests that without some
metaphysical confidence in an ultimate reality higher
than that of human experience, we can have no
grounds for believing that "we are not just making it up
when we have this sentiment of safety and belonging."
Yet this is not necessarily so, on logical no less than
psychological grounds. It seems to me that if someone
says "I have a strong sense of belonging here," we
must allow for the possibility that they might be
deceiving us, for one reason or another.[37] But if we
allow that possibility we must allow equally the
possibility that they are telling the truth. If such is the
case, then we cannot, on logical grounds, say of them
that they are engaged in self-deception, or are "just
making it up." I would hope that Huston might give
some sympathy to my position here, if not an
endorsement.

For some, abstract metaphysical engagement
may well be efficacious, indeed necessary, and on
this score I would "let a hundred flowers bloom." But
until very different, less transcendental (and more
plausible) metaphysics and theologies are put forth,
we might well follow the advice of Confucius when
asked whether the spirits of the ancestors were present
at the ritual sacrifices to them: "Sacrifice to the spirits
as though the spirits are present" (3.12). Attending to
this ancient Chinese wisdom can help us understand
in a different way the lines from Alexander Pope,
which, apart from the sexist language, I commend to
you:

Know then thyself, presume not God to scan;
The proper study of mankind is man

I have enjoyed this evening greatly; thank you very
much.

Epilogue

TO THE READER WHO HAS COME THIS FAR it will be apparent, I fear, that my responses to the issues and concerns raised by Huston Smith and by the audience are woefully incomplete. This fear was brought home to me by the several friends and colleagues acknowledged in the Preface, who individually and collectively suggested—graciously but firmly—that a number of my claims required amplification and/or further justification if they were to command a reader's attention in the pages of a small book. Hence this Epilogue.

One set of issues clustered around my views of science: how I see modern in relation to earlier science in the West; how I see science in other traditions; and how I see science in relation to metaphysics, especially the metaphysics found in religious texts. It is necessary for me to say more about these matters in order to make clearer my stronger claim that we can take the sacred texts of the world's religions as instructive for our lives without accepting the specific metaphysical (and theological) views and beliefs embedded in each of those texts. And finally, I need to expand somewhat my optimism for believing that those texts can contribute to the discipline of ego-reduction necessary for the kinds of religious experiences I have described when we are living in an increasingly self-centered, consumer-oriented, highly competitive capitalist society that threatens to engulf the whole world.

Science first. In one sense modern Western science is deeply indebted to its Greek ancestors, that sense being the assumption of an underlying reality—matter, substance—that beget the world of appearances, an ever-changing world. (The Chinese did not make this assumption, a theme to which I'll return below).

In most other respects, however, ancient and modern Western science are rather different. Contemporary practitioners of the several scientific disciplines clearly delineate a domain of data which they take as their task to explain; embrace a theoretical perspective that is both productive and constraining; they engage in extremely close observations—aided by highly sophisticated technology—of experiments designed to isolate and control variables; and they narrate the results of their efforts in quantitative statements. Further, relatively little of this work is motivated simply by the desire to learn more about how the world happens to be. Rather is the thrust of research to learn to manipulate the world more efficiently: nobly, by finding a cure for AIDS, or malaria; commercially, to find a better beauty cream to hide wrinkles; and more base, to create deadly chemical or biological weapons of war.

Most ancient Greek philosophers did not engage in these practices. "True opinion" (about the world of appearances) was, for Socrates and Plato, decidedly inferior to knowledge (of unchanging reality), which was to be obtained by dialectical reasoning, not observation and experiment.[38] While Aristotle took the empirical world more seriously than his teachers, he, too, was far more concerned with the conceptual—the syllogism, causality, form, and so on—than with the observational or experimental.[39] And the underlying question of all of their intellectual efforts was, I would maintain, not one that we look to modern science to answer today, namely, what is the best life for human beings?

I do not intend this comparison of ancient Greek and modern Western science as an invidious one; it is, after all, on the basis of modern science that I have argued for the bracketing of the cosmological and ontological—that is, metaphysical—statements found in the sacred texts and narratives of the world's religions. Except for method, however, modern Western science has by no means been monolithic: there are a large number of metaphysical views found in the history of modern science, many of which are incompatible with each other. If we can appreciate how and why this is so, perhaps we can come to also appreciate how and why scientific efforts are not threatening to religion.

One issue that bears equally on science, metaphysics, and religion will be well known to everyone who has taken an introductory philosophy course: the mind-body problem. As we understand it today, the problem originates with Descartes. There has been some speculation about why he was so obsessed with the issue of certainty, from whence the mind-body problem arose. It has been argued that

Descartes was traumatized by the assassination of Henry of Navarre, and the subsequent Thirty Years' War in which he was involved, and which included theological disputes such as the "true" nature of transubstantiation.[40] Others have speculated that the young René was frustrated deeply by a mathematical problem he could not solve, the frustration arising from the fact that deduction proceeds by a series of small, incremental steps, each of which should be clearly and distinctly obvious from the prior step.[41]

While taking both of these speculations seriously, it is also entirely possible that Descartes was simply continuing the ancient Greek tradition of attempting to conceptually reconcile the facts of change apparent to the senses on the one hand, and the fact that nature nevertheless conforms to itself on the other, by positing a substantial reality underlying the apparent changes, whether that substance was the water of Thales, the fire of Heraclitus, or the atoms of Democritus and Lucretius.

By meditating long and hard, Descartes discovered two substances, mind (that which thinks), and body (that which is extended). In keeping with the best scientific traditions of his day, however, and with respect for Occam's Razor, substances, whatever they were, had to be irreducible to other substances, and hence could not interact. Thus Descartes's problem, the legacy of which remains with us today: what is the relation between mind and body? Spinoza attempted to solve—or dissolve—the problem by going to the

extreme of arguing for only one substance, with
different modes and attributes. Leibniz went to the
other extreme, arguing for an indefinitely large number
of substances: his beloved monads, which, although
they could not interact, could nonetheless dance
beautifully in a preestablished harmony to music
composed by God.

Science and philosophy parted company at this
time, for already in Leibniz's day the concept of body—
matter, substance—had undergone a profound change.
Descartes also posited "subtle matter," which could
provide a strictly mechanical account of heat, light,
gravity, electricity, magnetism, celestial motion, and
much else. Movement through this "subtle matter"—
later, "aether"—was transmitted by physical
contact, which could alter both speed and direction.

Newton's equations, however, required that
bodies—substance, matter, (subtle or otherwise) be
capable of affecting each other without being in any
physical contact, dooming the moving bodies, matter-
in-motion, billiard-ball Cartesian mechanical universe
once and for all. Newton himself, in the well-known
quote, "feigned no hypotheses" about how this action-
at-a-distance, occult phenomenon could take place
(which is the major reason Leibniz was so reluctant to
accept Newton's results); but henceforward, "body"
could no longer mean for scientists what it had meant
to Descartes.

His notion of "subtle matter" was not altogether
abandoned for over two centuries, but as the "aether,"

it, too, changed and was developed until Einstein's equations permitted a very different explanation of the results of the Michaelson-Morley experiments (which supposedly showed that the speed of light particles was not impeded by the aether).

In addition to body and aether, other concepts were invented, changed, and developed by scientists: the "humours," for example, helped explain the workings of the human body for Harvey in a different way than for Hippocrates. A new subtle body—phlogiston—was introduced to account for combustion. Like aether, these latter terms are no longer found in the scientific literature; now, we are told, *real* bodies are ever-so-wee-things, fermions.

Someday, perhaps, fermions will go the way of phlogiston, and perhaps space—another term whose meaning has changed over time—will turn out not to be curved in Riemannian fashion, but good old-fashioned Euclidean after all. But what is significant, I think, is that while employing terms like "aether," "phlogiston," and "humours" in redefining the meaning of "body," or "matter," scientists have given us invaluable insights into the natural world we inhabit, even as many of these terms later gave way to others.

Thus, for myself, I am happy to let scientists define "body" in whatever way it suits them, and to tell me how I should use the term, if not in everyday parlance, then at the least in technical philosophical discourse.[42]

Turning now to the other term, "mind," I have no truck with reductionistic efforts to translate the language of mental states into the language of brain (body) states. Reductionism is a tried and true methodology in the natural sciences, the mathematical results of which have high predictive value. But at least for the foreseeable future, it will remain that the lexicon of mental terms serves a very different explanatory function than the language of physical (body) terms.

It must be noted that while the study of the brain—as physical body—belongs to the natural sciences, the study of the mind is the purview of the social and behavioral sciences, which, owing to the complexity of the human mind, is a major reason for their still not being truly worthy of being considered sciences. Differing concepts of mind can differentiate disciplines, and theories within them.

For economists, and some political scientists, the mind is an exquisite machine for calculating self-interest among competing possibilities (an ego-enhancing concept). For most anthropologists and sociologists, it is the mechanism whereby one's behavior is integrated with the behavior of others (ditto). Freudians ascribe both subconscious and unconscious dimensions to the mind, and point to a power to suppress and repress parts of itself (ditto again). Other psychologists of a Skinnerian bent insist that a concept of mind is unnecessary to develop a science of behavior. Chomskyan linguists describe the mind as modular, with highly specific cognitive capacities, triggered into activity by environmental stimuli rather than being shaped by them.

The results of these social and behavioral investigations, described in mentalistic language, but with differing conceptions of the mind, have been fairly meager in aiding our understanding of the world in which we live when compared to the natural (bodily) sciences, and have made it much more difficult for us to be open to religious experience, but they have not been inconsequential; we do now know more about the dynamics of our lives as individuals, and as members of communities, than our ancestors did, and this knowledge did not come about because of our notion of body: concepts of friendship, power, honor, shame, love, guilt, oppression, dignity, values, and much more, are all essential for understanding what it is to be human, and the appropriate language for communicating this knowledge is mentalistic from start to finish.

For these reasons, I will bow to the social and behavioral scientists in allowing them to define mind as they differentially wish, just as I bowed earlier to the natural scientists with respect to body. I will not bow anywhere near as deeply, of course, because the former do not speak with one mind, and hence each should remain open to comments and criticisms from practitioners of the other disciplines, and from philosophers and other humanists as well, especially with regard to what they have to say about religion.

It thus appears to me that the concept of body has evolved considerably in the natural sciences over the past three centuries, and there is currently no generally accepted theory of the mind in the social and behavioral sciences, and I conclude from these observations that no sufficiently precise definitions of either mind or body can be given to clearly formulate a problem concerning their relation to each other.[43]

Clearly my reading of the history of modern Western science requires attentiveness not only to cultural, but also to temporal context, which shows that scientists have frequently changed their minds about what there was, and was not, in the universe they studied. Thus, if my reading of that history is a plausible one, a number of inferences can be drawn from it.

The first of these inferences recapitulates one of Huston's claims: although it does not today speak of differing levels of reality, tomorrow's science may postulate such, perhaps even to include a transcendental realm. I personally am agnostic with respect to such metaphysical claims, but the thrust of my reply to Huston is that such claims are not *necessary* in order to argue for continuing to take most seriously the sacred texts and narratives of the world's traditions.

And as with the transcendent, so too with the teleological. Western scientists used to employ the terms "purpose" and "purposive" regularly in their accounts of God's handiwork, not radically different from their use of "phlogiston" or "aether" except for the level of abstraction involved. But old ideas may return—think of the atoms of Democritus, the heliocentric views of Aristarchus—especially in the social and behavioral sciences: many insights might be gained by asking what the goal of human society is, or what purposes persons might have; such questions are perhaps too important to be entrusted solely to philosophers and theologians.

There are other reasons why I have discussed the so-called "mind-body problem" at some length; indeed I want to discuss it further, now in a cross-cultural context. In my lecture I argued that we will most productively reread the religious texts of our own traditions if we read carefully the texts of other traditions at the same time. And I would maintain that scientific and philosophical texts should be reread in the same way.

If the mind-body problem is a universal one, it should be found in other traditions that have what can legitimately be considered science and philosophy. China most assuredly has both, but no mind-body "problem" is ever considered in the writings of its philosophers and scientists.

Simply put, there are no simple terms in the lexicon of ancient Chinese for "mind" or "body"—or Greek *soma* for that matter—sufficiently approximating the English terms to effect a clear translation of the "problem," even if those terms are taken solely in their ordinary, everyday senses.

Body first. The Chinese expression *wan wu* is usually translated as "the ten thousand things," and the translation is not misleading so long as we remember that the English "things" does not always refer to material objects. It does in expressions like "fools and things, cabbages and kings," but shifts somewhat in the famous quote from Rebecca West, "Art does not copy the world; one of the damned thing is enough." In the old song, "These Foolish Things Remind Me of You," half of the items cataloged—sounds, smells, memories— are not substantial, and we all know and understand fully the keen observation that "the best things in life aren't things."

For over two hundred years another Chinese expression, *wu xing*, has been rendered as the "five elements," and it is understandable why this was done, because the quintet referred to was made up of metal, wood, fire, earth, and water. But *xing* doesn't mean "element" in any way remotely resembling the Greek "Four Elements" theory. The proper translation for *wu xing* is "five phases."

Insisting on the accuracy of translation here is not an exercise in etymological nitpicking. In order to comprehend the early Chinese view of the cosmos, the good earth, and the place of human beings therein it is necessary to attempt to see, feel, understand the world as not so much made up of substances, matters, bodies—nouns—but rather as series of events, processes, relations. Consider the following statement from Nathan Sivin:

> Scientific thought began, in China as elsewhere, with attempts to comprehend how it is that although individual things are constantly changing, always coming to be and perishing, nature as a coherent order not only endures but remains conformable to itself. In the West the earliest such attempts identified the unchanging reality with some basic stuff out of which all the things around us, despite their apparent diversity, are formed. In China the earliest and in the long run the most influential scientific explanations were in terms of time. They made sense of the momentary event by fitting it into the cyclical rhythms of natural process.[44]

(It can be noted in passing that perhaps one reason the Chinese focused on time in their sciences is that they did not have any revelatory affirmation that the how and why of the universe could be ultimately intelligible to human beings, and hence were more concerned with temporal regularities found in nature than with explanations grounded in the supernatural.)

I would extend Sivin's cogent account to include not only scientific, but Chinese moral and religious descriptions, analyses, and evaluations as well. The basic "stuff"—body, matter, substance, the underlying reality that is unchanging—of the scientific West is conceptually analogous to the enduring self ("strict self-identity"), or soul, of the moral and religious West. The Chinese, on the other hand, made sense of personal identity "by fitting it into the cyclical rhythms of natural process." Many factors enter into the analysis of benefactor-beneficiary roles in Confucianism, but time is essential.[45]

When we hear someone say, "I'm not the person I used to be," we interpret the statement as a lament on the aging process. For the Chinese, however, the statement would be quite literally true. When young I was a beneficiary of my parents and elders, now I am their benefactor. Marriage made me a different person, and becoming a parent changed me even more, as did entry into grandfatherhood. Divorce would make me yet different again, and one day I will be beneficiary of my children, no longer a benefactor. Of course through all of these cyclic, temporal changes I have a body, but what kind of body? Sivin once more:

> In China the boundaries of the [human] body were different than in Greece. The terms normally used for the body, *shen*, and *ti*, cover a great deal more than Greek *somai*, which clearly denotes the physical. *Shen* includes the individual personality, and may refer in a general way to the person, rather than to the body. *Ti* refers to the concrete physical body. . . . It can also mean "embodiment," and may refer to an individual's personification of something. *Chu* comes closer to the scope of the European notion of body, but *ling chu* implies the person, and *chu* was not a common word. The only term for the body that has nothing to do with the person seen whole, *xing*, literally means "shape." It often refers to the body's outline rather than to its physical identity. It is not surprising that the European mind-body dichotomy (among a great many other mental habits) seems exotic to East Asians . . . [46]

Thus the ancient Chinese did not have Cartesian bodies. They didn't have Cartesian minds either. Unlike the numerous Chinese graphs that may be translated as "body" on occasion, there is only one rendered as "mind": *xin*; originally a stylized picture of the aorta, it is the seat of thought. But there's a catch: it is also the seat of feeling. The *xin* equally reasons, reflects, hopes, fears, and desires. Thus there is no sharp cognitive/affective split in early Chinese thought, not because of any naiveté or epistemological astigmatism on their part, but rather to their not postulating a larger mind/body ontology of which the cognitive/affective dichotomy is a logical corollary.[47]

I hope this lengthy excursus into differing concepts of mind and body, both in Western science and philosophy, and in China, will make clearer my arguments for approaching religious texts in a different way, and more important, why I have attempted to frame those arguments without making metaphysical commitments. My major claim is that the sacred texts and narratives are all describing similar spiritual disciplines to follow in order to be open to religious experiences, which also appear to be very similar across time, place, language, and culture. But: those descriptions all employ symbols, metaphors, and descriptions of the world that are grounded in temporally and culturally specific metaphysical views (whether always made explicit in the texts, or not). Hence I am obliged to conclude that no *specific* set of metaphysical views or beliefs is necessary for everyone to hold in order to follow a spiritual path and be open to the kinds of religious experiences that countless numbers of adherents of every tradition have had throughout history.

This is a general philosophical claim on my part, fairly abstract. Even if it be accepted, it does not adequately warrant my seemingly more radical—because counterintuitive—claim that specific metaphysical and theological views and beliefs are not necessary in order to gain insight into the nature of paths to religious experience from the text(s) which are defined by these specific metaphysical and theological views and beliefs.

But think, for example, of grains and grapes, products of the earth, which, with individual and collective human effort, provide food and drink necessary to sustain our human lives, and thereby link us irrevocably to this (increasingly fragile) good earth. One might come to feel this link at any time, in any culture, perhaps when partaking of bread or wine. Yet that sense of "linkage"—a weaker but not inconsequential form of "belonging"—will almost surely come more easily to those who attend carefully to the demonstrative pronouns within the tradition that sacralizes the statements "This is my body; this is my blood."

Now I ask, not altogether rhetorically, are these statements utterly devoid of significance for those unwilling or unable to accept the theological—and hence metaphysical—claim that Jesus Christ is the Son of God? Couldn't these statements contribute to generating a sense of at-one-ment for those who hold different theological beliefs, or who hold no such beliefs whatsoever? The answer, of course, is "No" if the statements are only read literally, that is, directly (think of Oppenheimer again). And at the extreme, such readers may well find repellent a tradition that insists on ritual cannibalism as one of its highest sacraments, as I suggested earlier. (Think of the Hindu goddess Kali again).

But I want to go further in deemphasizing the importance of the specific metaphysical and theological underpinnings of each of the world's religions when studying their sacred texts and narratives. Consider again the transcendental realm, central to the Abrahamic heritage. By focusing on this realm as a reality wholly other than the reality we experience in our daily lives, we focus simultaneously on the radical otherness of God, and the divinity of Christ. On this God we are dependent without remainder for our lives, and our eternal future; when he "calls" us, we die. We trust that if we follow the Good Book faithfully we will be rewarded; but no matter how hard we strive, such reward is not guaranteed. We cannot command God in any way, but must, in the end, rely on His love, and His grace, for a desired hereafter.

With such metaphysics and theology uppermost in our minds, it will obviously be more difficult to have the kinds of religious experience I have described, the experience of belonging, of safety, of at-one-ment or attunement, in and with the world of our everyday lives. Equally or even more important, a preoccupation with the transcendental realm makes it extremely difficult to appreciate what the Incarnation and the Passion of Christ actually signifies: God is *in,* and of, this world He created. (For myself, within the Christian tradition, the healthiest antidote to the over-transcendentalizing of God is the writings of Julian of Norwich).[48]

Similar arguments apply to other religious traditions. Hindus and Buddhists preoccupied with the ontological dimensions of *karma* and *dharma* may miss an important message the South Asian sacred texts convey: that we alone are responsible for our place in a world not of our making, and for our responses to it; if the world brings us sorrow, it is up to us, not the world, to alleviate the sorrow, and to come to terms with that world.

Non-Muslims will similarly misunderstand Islam if Mohammed is taken as the counterpart of Jesus. If the Christian God enters the lived world through His son, Allah enters the world through his words, as dictated to his Prophet and recorded in the Quran (which is why reciting that text is a sacrament for Muslims, and also why there can be no authentic translation of it).[49] These examples, and many others that might be proffered in brief compass, may well not sway a skeptic convinced that a religious text can only provide guidance for leading more meaningful lives to those who accept its metaphysical and theological assumptions or presuppositions. My examples, it might be objected, can either be seen as anecdotal, or as my simply reading out of specific passages in specific texts a number of ideas by which I have already been seized.

I should therefore like to examine a specific text more systematically, describing a path that can lead to spiritual experience, a path that may commend itself to people with a wide range of metaphysical or theological views and beliefs, or who have none at all, a path that dichotomizes neither the lived from a transcendental world, nor minds from bodies, nor ourselves from others, or from the lived world.

My text is the *Analects* of Confucius. I chose it not only because it is one with which I have had a long and close association, but also because it can be read as containing no explicit metaphysics, and nothing affirmed in the text conflicts in any way with the pronouncements of modern science.[50]

In the *Analects* Confucius and at times his disciples make approbatory remarks about several kinds of persons, three of which I want to focus on: the *shi* or "scholar-apprentice," *junzi*, "exemplary person," and *sheng* or *shengren*, "sage," contrasting these three with the *xiaoren*, "petty person."

All three of these expressions were in use before the time of Confucius. In the *Book of Songs*, for example, the term *shi* is used for a man of middle social status, at other times for a retainer, and yet again to designate a servant. It also appeared to be the term for a lower-level functionary of a lord, perhaps a man of arms, somewhat akin to the old English knight (and Waley so translates the term). A *junzi* was a lord's son, or perhaps the bastard son of a lord. The character *sheng* in the *Book of Documents* would appear to have the meaning of "very wise person."

Confucius appropriated all of these terms for his own use, giving them connotations and denotations that shifted their sense and reference away from position, rank, birth, or function toward what we (not he) would term aesthetic, moral, and spiritual characteristics. Owing to Kierkegaard and others, these three areas of human concern are distinct realms in the West; their interrelatedness would be self-evident to Confucius. The sacred is not transcendentally distinct from the secular in China.

Twelve passages in the *Analects* make reference to the *shi*, most of which suggest that they are apprentices of some kind. The *shi* are to be precise and formal, punctilious perhaps. They have already extended themselves beyond the family, for in no passages in the *Analects* is *xiao*—filial piety—associated with the *shi*. Moreover, while the structure of the twelve passages has suggested to most translators that what is being described are the *shi*'s qualities—that is, what they are—I believe those passages are better construed as instructions for what the *shi* should do. They have set out on a path, a road, but they still have a long way to go, and there is much yet to be done. As Master Zeng says (8.7):

Scholar-apprentices *(shi)* cannot but be strong and
resolved, for they bear a heavy charge and the way *(dao)*
is long. Where they take authoritative conduct *(ren)* as
their charge, is it not a heavy one? And where their way
ends only in death, is it not indeed long?

By describing the *shi* as one who has assumed
the burden of *ren*, we get a strong hint that it is a
moral and spiritual apprenticeship the *shi* are serving,
for *ren* is the highest excellence for Confucius. Further
evidence that the *shi* is one who has set out on a
spiritual path is found elsewhere (4.9 and 14.2) in
which negative instructions are given, the thrust of
which is to eschew material well-being.

There are, of course, numerous positive
instructions the Master proffers, not only for the *shi*,
but for others as well: become steeped in poetry
(16.13), and in history (3.14); study and practice the
rituals (12.20); listen to, play, become absorbed in
music (3.23); perform public service when it is
appropriate to do so (13.20); and above all—and by so
engaging in these efforts—learn to extend one's human
sympathies beyond the family, clan, and village
(13.28), and learn to become benefactor and
beneficiary within a much larger circle. Again, the *shi*
are never instructed in the proper behavior and
demeanor due one's parents, children, or other
relatives; more is needed:

> Zizhang said, "Those *shi* are quite acceptable who on
> seeing danger are ready to put their lives on the line,
> who on seeing an opportunity for gain concern

themselves with what is appropriate, who in performing sacrifice concern themselves with proper respect and who in participating in a funeral concern themselves with grief." (19.1)

If my reading of these passages is warranted, it will follow that the major goal toward which the *shi* is striving is to become an exemplary person, or *junzi*. The *shi* does, while the *junzi* more nearly *is*. In the text, the *junzi* is almost always described (for the benefit of the disciples), not instructed (because presumably they don't need it). They have traveled a goodly distance along the way, and live a goodly number of roles. Benefactor to many, they are still beneficiaries of others like themselves. While still capable of anger in the presence of inappropriateness and concomitant injustice, they are in their persons tranquil. They know many rituals and much music, and perform all of their functions not only with skill, but also with grace, dignity, and beauty, and take delight in the performances. Still filial toward parents and elders, they now take "all under *tian*" as their dwelling place. While real enough to be still capable of the occasional lapse in their otherwise exemplary conduct (14.6), they are resolutely proper in the conduct of their roles—conduct which is not forced, but rather effortless, spontaneous, creative. There is, in sum, a very strong aesthetic and ethical dimension to this life; *junzi* have reauthorized the *li*—rituals—and therefore become respected authors of the *dao* of humankind.[51]

For most of us, the goal of *junzi* is the highest to which we can aspire. There is, however, an even loftier human goal, to become a "sage" or *shengren*; but in the *Analects* it is a distant goal indeed.

There are eight references to *shengren* in the text. In one passage, Confucius dares not rank himself a *shengren* (7.34), in another he laments that he never has, and probably never will, meet one (7.26), and in still another he gently chastises Zigong when the latter likens him to a *shengren* (9.6). And later, even though Mencius allows that the man in the street who acts like a Yao or a Shun (that is, a *shengren*) is a sage, he, too, suggests strongly that this goal is beyond the reach of most mortals (6b2).

Yet it is there. There are *shengren*. They have risen beyond the level of *junzi*, because 16.8 describes *junzi* as those who stand in awe of the words of the *shengren*. From 6.30 we learn that one who confers benefits on and assists everyone is a *shengren*.

And finally, Zixia allows that it is not even the *junzi*, but the *shengren* alone "who walks this path every step from start to finish" (19.12), beginning with what was near, and getting to what was distant (14.35). If the career of Confucius is one example of sagehood, perhaps walking the path from start to finish reports on Confucius himself, who, at the end of his life, could give his "heart-and-mind free rein without overstepping the boundaries" (2.4).

To summarize this brief reading of the qualities of, and relations between, the *shi*, the *junzi*, and the *shengren*: all *shengren* are *junzi*, and all *junzi* were formerly *shi*, but the converse does not hold. These are, in other words, ranked types of persons, and the ranking is based on a progression from scholarly apprenticeship to sagehood. *Shi* are, relatively speaking, fairly numerous, *junzi* are more scarce, and *sheng* are very few and far between, owing to the "heaviness of the burden, and the distance of the journey" (8.7).

The *shi* are resolute in following the *dao* as it is embodied in custom, tradition, and ritual propriety (*li*) that govern the interpersonal relations definitive of the *shi*'s several roles. Much farther along this journey of learning and doing we have the *junzi*, who know the *li* thoroughly enough to express its spirit even in the absence of precedent; they perform their roles masterfully, and derive a deep satisfaction from the grace, dignity, effortlessness, and creativity with which they have come to conduct themselves with others, strangers no less than kin. And it is the *junzi* who ascend in the midst of many to provide a bearing for exemplary conduct through effective service in roles of social and political responsibility.

At the upper end of this continuum are the *shengren*. In addition to possessing all of the qualities of the *junzi*, the *shengren* appear to see and feel custom, rituals, and traditions holistically, as defining and integrating the human community broadly, and as defining and integrating as well the communities of the past, and of the future. This seeing and feeling of the *shengren* can be described as an awareness which gives one the capacity to go beyond the particular time and place in which we live, effecting a continuity not only with our contemporaries, but with those who have preceded us, and with those who will follow after us; that is to say, a strong sense of belonging, of safety, of at-one-ment, attunement, with all of our fellow human beings.

The metaphors used to describe the *shengren* are cosmic and celestial: "Confucius is the sun and moon which no one can climb beyond" (19.24). The culture that finds its focus in this rare person elevates the human experience to heights of profound aesthetic, moral, and religious refinement, making the human being a worthy partner with the heavens and the earth. The model of the *shengren* shines across generations and across geographical boundaries as a light that not only stabilizes and secures the human world, but that also serves humankind as a source of cultural nourishment and inspiration. It is the *shengren* who leads the way of the human being (*ren dao*) into its more certain future.

In reading the relationship between the *shi, junzi,* and *shengren* hierarchically, it must be emphasized that the hierarchy should not just be imagined vertically, concluding in a transcendent we-know-not-what. Rather do I want to maintain the rich path imagery of *dao* in the *Analects*: the *shengren* have traveled, appropriated, and enlarged a longer stretch of the road than the *shi* and *junzi*, and they are providing signposts and a bearing for the latter as well. And to follow that road is to engage in an ego-reducing spiritual discipline.

This is a woefully brief account of the major spiritual discipline of the early Confucians, a path that integrates the aesthetic, the moral, and the socio-political with the religious. As we follow that path, we will be led to see ourselves less as free, autonomous, unchanging selves/souls, less as altogether distinct from the physical world, and more as co-members of a multiplicity of communities, who, through sustained effort, are increasingly integrated into an ever-larger community, something larger than ourselves. We must come to see and feel ourselves as fundamentally, not accidentally, intergenerationally bound to our ancestors, contemporaries, and descendants. It is not that we are to become selfless, i.e., altruistic, for this would imply an isolated self to be surrendered, the pure existence of which any Confucian must deny; rather must we come to see and feel our personhood as dependent on others for its uniqueness, just as others must depend on us for their uniqueness: in order to be a friend, or a lover, I must *have* a friend or lover; and "freedom" must be seen not as a state of being, but as an achievement for each of us. So long as I feel I *must* meet my defining obligations I am obviously not free. Only when I come to want to meet them, enjoy doing so, and come to feel at-one-ment with my fellows past, present, and future, can I enjoy true freedom, and make spiritual progress in both the social and natural worlds.

Following such a path clearly involves ego-reduction, and the promise of the religious experience of belonging, in the case of the *Analects*, to and with the human community. Had I chosen the *Dao De Jing*, the ego-reducing path would lead more to a sense of safety, of attunement with the natural world. And we may read Buddhist, Hindu, and other sacred texts and narratives in similar ways.

But I chose to elaborate the Way of the *Analects* because the concept of the person found therein is the most contrastive with the concept of autonomous individual selves/souls that have tended to dominate the Abrahamic traditions, especially since the Enlightenment period and the rise of industrial capitalism, and also because it speaks not of a transcendental realm nor of anything inconsistent with the pronouncements of contemporary science.[52]

Everyone in the West with eyes to see is aware of the manifold problems attendant on an altogether individualistic orientation, but I do not believe we take those problems seriously enough at the conceptual or experiential level. First-generation human rights, for example, grounded in the concept of freely choosing autonomous individuals, may indeed offer some protection from the whims of despotic governments, but they also serve to maintain a gross and growing misdistribution of the world's wealth, they provide legal justification for transnational corporations to do as they wish, and they have led to an increasing loss of community. Relatedly, as autonomous individuals, it is extremely difficult for us to contemplate seriously that there may be a higher good independent of our conception of it, and we will continue to insist, in the public sphere at least, that justice continue to be defined procedurally rather than distributively. Worse, as autonomous individuals, "they"—the Other—all too easily become radically other, and even "we"—those very similar to us—become Other in a capitalist society wherein competition is the norm in a series of zero-sum games; if you get the golden ring, I do not.

Whether we are ultimately autonomous individuals or co-members of the human community is of course not an empirical question, and I know of no conclusive rational argument for one or the other, a priori or otherwise. Worse, these differing views are in many ways self-prophetic; the more we believe ourselves to be essentially autonomous individuals, the more easily we become such. This view is very deeply rooted in contemporary Western culture, especially in the U.S., and in my opinion is largely responsible for much of the malaise increasingly definitive of it. In this sense classical Confucian spirituality proffers a radical alternative view of the world and our place in it, but for all that, I believe it is a viable one. We *are* the offspring of our parents; we are siblings, neighbors, students, lovers, parents, spouses, friends, and much else of an interpersonal nature. The Confucian vision does not shrink the personal human sprit by isolating it as a self-contained atom, but rather enlarges it by linking it to all other human spirits, and with the natural world whose spirit equally animates us all.

Moreover, this Confucian vision of relatedness may also assist us in overcoming an altogether materialistic orientation—personal and metaphysical—toward that natural world that makes the sense of belonging in it far more difficult to achieve. Science describes that natural world, but does not contradict the view expressed not only in the *Analects* but in all sacred texts: we do not live by bread alone.

TO CONCLUDE by way of reiteration: comparative religious studies have been largely a Western intellectual endeavor, and hence it is not surprising that the Abrahamic tradition has been taken as paradigmatic of religion. Thus when examining other traditions it has been common to ask what the inheritors thereof believe with respect to how the world came to be, is, and will be, which I believe is a misguided approach, for virtually all such claims in every tradition cannot be made to square with contemporary science. This focus, resting on the affirmation that the universe is ultimately intelligible to us—that the "why?" questions all have answers— generates a reading of the Abrahamic and other texts that focus in turn on the question of the meaning of life.

But by reading these texts to learn how they all describe paths to follow for finding meaning *in* life, meaning may indeed be found. That meaning will very probably not be a godly or cosmic meaning, but a human one; which would not, however, be inconsequential, for human is what we are.

NOTES

About these notes:

(1) Terms, persons, places, quotes, and facts that are commonplace are not referenced below; to have done so would make this section much longer than all of the others combined.

(2) Biblical references are to the Expanded Edition of the *Oxford Annotated Bible,* Revised Standard Version.

(3) References to the Confucian *Analects* are to the translation by Roger Ames and me (Ballantine, 1998).

(4) Books cited that are followed by an asterisk (*) are suggested as further reading for those interested in pursuing further the major themes I have all too briefly taken up herein.

1. On a number of issues, however, I have expanded on my arguments in the Discussion and Epilogue sections, and in these notes.

2. *Forgotten Truth** (HarperSanFrancisco, 1992), p. 107.

3. In addition to Huston Smith, other scholars of comparative religions have also argued that the similarities among and between the world's religions are more significant than their differences. See, for example, Mircea Eliade, trans. W. Trask, *The Sacred and the Profane** (Harper & Row, 1961); Frithjof Schuon, *The Transcendental Unity of Religions* (Harper & Row, 1975); and of course the classic of William James, *The Varieties of Religious Experience** (Mentor, 1958). In arguing their cases, however, all of these scholars employ ontological assumptions I am reluctant to rely upon defending my claim.

4. This claim was first made by S. N. Balagangadhara in '*The Heathen in His Blindness . . .': Asia and The West and the Dynamic of Religion* (E. J. Brill, 1994). See also my "How Do You Learn to Be Religious?" as a response to this book, in *Cultural Dynamics* 8, no. 3 (July, 1996).

5. Creation stories do not begin to appear in China until the early Han Dynasty, well over a century after the classical period of Chinese thought (sixth through the third centuries B.C.E.) ends.

6. In the several schools of Hinduism, the concept of *maya* does not entail that the world we perceive is basically illusory; what is illusory is that many features of the perceived world appear to have a permanence about them which they do not have. For Buddhists and the doctrine of co-dependent origination, this applies to the world *tout court*.

7. See note 4.

8. *Tractatus*, 6.522 (Pears and McGuiness translation; Routledge & Kegan Paul, 1961)

9. For specific citations regarding Kierkegaard here and following, see my "Kierkegaard & Confucius: On Following the Way" in *Philosophy East and West* 36, no. 3 (July, 1986). There and herein I have profited from John Douglas Mullen's *Kierkegaard's Philosophy: Self-Deception and Cowardice in the Present Age** (Mentor, 1981).

10. For further reflections on this theme, and for excerpts from a number of other writers, see Herbert Fingarette's meditation

(and anthology) *Death: Philosophical Soundings* (Open Court Pub. Co., 1996).

11. See James, op. cit, especially Lextures XVI and XVII.

12. For an analysis of the religious dimensions of the concept of "Experience," see the essay of that name by Robert H. Sharf in *Critical Terms for Religious Studies*, edited by Mark Taylor (University of Chicago Press, 1997). As should be clear from my text, I do not endorse Sharf's skepticism about the possibility of usefully employing the term in religious studies research. The most clear, and to my mind most useful brief work on the mystical experience remains W.T. Stace's Introduction to his *Teachings of the Mystics** (Mentor, 1960). For an account of psychology's contribution—or lack of it—to any understanding of mysticism, see Frits Staal, *Exploring Mysticism* (Univ. of California Press, 1975). In *Civilization and Its Discontents* (Norton, 1961), Freud describes what he takes to be religious experience as an "oceanic feeling," and is obviously suspicious of the mystical; see especially pp. 14–20. For further philosophical discussion of mysticism I would recommend Sallie B. King's "Two Epistemological Models for the Interpretation of Mysticism" and Huston's "Is There a Perennial Philosophy?" both of which appear in the *Journal of the American Academy of Religion* (Smith's is in vol. 55, no. 3, King's in vol. 56, no. 2). Both King and Smith challenge the analysis of mysticism proffered in the writings of Steven B. Katz, who responds to these two critical essays in vol. 56, no. 4, which is followed by rejoinders from his two critics. I wish the "eating the menu instead of the dinner" was my own, but it originated with Alan Watts, *The Way of Zen* (Pantheon, 1957), p. xi, paraphrasing William James, op. cit.: "offering a printed bill of fare as the equivalent for a solid meal" (p. 377).

13. For the Confucian orientation to this linkage, see the now-classic *Confucius—The Secular as Sacred** by Herbert Fingarette (Harper & Row, 1972).

14. An excellent overview of the extent to which this path permeates all of Confucianism for over two millennia is Philip J. Ivanhoe, *Confucian Moral Self-Cultivation* (Hackett Pub. Co., 2nd ed., 2000). See also note 50, below.

15. See Note 11, and Stace, op. cit. The purely mystical experience seems regularly, but not always, to eventuate in the kind of religious experience which is my focus.

16. On this score, see especially Roger T. Ames, "Bushido: Mode or Ethic?" in *Japanese Aesthetics and Culture*, ed. Nancy G. Hume (SUNY Press, 1995).

17. For myself, the best edition of Thoreau's *Walden* for fully appreciating the text is Philip Van Doren Stern's *The Annotated Walden** (Clarkson Potter, Inc., 1970). *A Sand County Almanac** is by Aldo Leopold (Oxford Univ. Press, 1966), with many reprintings. Annie Dillard's *Pilgrim at Tinker Creek** was published by Harper & Row, 1974. Thomas Berry is author not only of *The Dream of the Earth** (Sierra Club, 1988), but the more recent *The Great Work** (Bell Tower, 1999).

18. But they say much about the meditative. Harold D. Roth, *Original Dao* (Columbia University Press, 1999), is the best introduction, in my mind, to this path in early Daoism.

19. In addition to their writings, all of these treaders of differing Catholic paths now have biographies as well.

20. See note 12.

21. Wittgenstein used the terms "mystical," "religious," and "ethical" almost interchangeably throughout his writings to signify all that was beyond "was der Fall ist" (*Tractatus* 1) and at times included the aesthetic as well: "Ethics and Aesthetics are one and the same" (*Tractatus* 6.421). Consider the following remarkable autobiographical statements, given in a lecture on ethics to Cambridge undergraduates:

> I believe the best way of describing [this experience of the ethical] is to say that when I have it *I wonder at the existence of the world*. . . .
> I will mention another experience straight away which I also know and which others of you might be acquainted with: it is, what one might call, the experience of feeling *absolutely* safe. I mean the state of mind in which one is inclined to say "I am safe, nothing can injure me whatever happens."

("Wittgenstein's Lecture on Ethics," in the *Philosophica Review* 74 (1965): 8; italics in the original). According to Ray Monk, Wittgenstein's most comprehensive biographer to date, Wittgenstein first got this notion of safety in early Vienna, watching a play by the Austrian dramatist Ludwig Anzengruber. Thereafter, according to Monk, "For the rest of his life he continued to regard the feeling of being "absolutely safe" as paradigmatic of religious experience." *Ludwig Wittgenstein: The Duty of Genius* (Free Press, 1990, p. 51). It should also be noted that in the lecture on ethics, Wittgenstein claimed that his statements about wonder and safety were "nonsense." To the best of my knowledge, William James was the first to link religious experience with "safety." See esp. op. cit., p. 367.

22. I am thinking here of such groups as those of Jim Jones in Guyana, the Branch Davidians of Texas, and the Heaven's Gate group of California, all of which reaped the whirlwind.

23. David Hall and Roger Ames have argued well and at length in a number of works on the uniqueness of the concept of a transcendental realm to the Western cultural tradition, beginning with their *Thinking Through Confucius** (Suny Press, 1987).

24. Noam Chomsky, *Powers and Prospects* (South End Press, 1996), p. 27.

25. "On Representing Abstractions in Archaic Chinese," in *Philosophy East and West* 24, no. 1 (January, 1974); "Against Relativism," in *Interpreting Across Boundaries*, ed. G. Larson and E. Deutsch (Princeton Univ. Press, 1987); and the Introduction and appendices to the *Analects* translation, op. cit.

26. The grammar of our native tongue influences our cognitive efforts in ways that are very difficult to change. Consider the following from the highly perceptive comparative philosopher Sallie B. King:

> Wittgenstein may have persuaded us that words have many other functions, but the fact remains that in everyday use we very frequently do use words to refer to things, and the very fact that when we speak of 'God' the surface grammar appears to make 'God' into a thing, results in a deeply ingrained conceptual habit. Hence my advocacy of the anti-concept.

("Concepts, Anti-Concepts, and Religious Experience" in *Religious Studies* 14 [19—]: 458). I commend King's notion of "anti-concepts" to the reader's attention, but here want to call attention to her footnote to this passage:

> If a confessional note be allowed by way of illustration, I have somehow arrived at the point where I think 'God' in association with

the grounding mystery, but when I hear or read the word 'God,' I immediately associate the word with a being, Our Father in Heaven. (*Ibid.*)

No such being dwells in the *tian* of Confucius, which is why I reject "heaven" as translation, and merely transliterate it.

27. To expand this point further: In the course of an incisive critique of the draft of my lecture, David Wong argued that I had underplayed the significance of the descriptions of the world proffered by the world's religions with respect to the *content* of the spiritual experiences obtained by the adherents thereof. (Private correspondence.) I do not at all wish to underplay the religious significance of those descriptions for the faithful, and am grateful to Wong for obliging me to say more on this point, which I attempt to do in the Epilogue.

28. And at times the not so naive as well. Kant, disparaging mysticism as something a person engages in "where his reason no longer understands itself and its own intentions," then attributes this engagement to Daoism, saying, "Out of this misbehavior the monster system of Laotse arises, teaching that the highest good consists in nothingness. . . . This nothingness, truly conceived, is a concept which annihilates all understanding and in which thought itself arrives at its end." Quoted from "Das Ende aller Dinge" by Richard Kroner in his *Kant's Weltanschauung*, trans. John Smith (Univ. of Chicago Press, 1956), pp. 15–16.

29. "Rationality" need not, of course, be applied only to those who accept the implausible affirmation of the full explanatory intelligibility of the world; if so applied, the majority of the human race would have to be classified as non- or ir-rational, myself included. Again following Chomsky, while I believe we can come to know much more about the world, there are limits on human understanding imposed by our mental and physical structures. At the top of my list of possible sciences not possible for human beings is a science of human motivation and behavior. Such a science—perhaps available to different forms of intelligent beings, constituted very differently than we are—would have to be able to describe and explain what is beyond human cognitive capacity; while tautologous, it can be important to say that what is beyond our capacity to think is beyond our capacity to think. Chomsky has

discussed this view cogently on a number of occasions, one source being his *Rules and Representations* (Columbia Univ. Press, 1980), pp. 251–53.

30. One of the most important of these resources is the sense of community, neighborhood, the importance of being in a place. For several excellent discussions of this theme, see *The Longing for Home*, ed. Leroy Rouner (Univ. of Notre Dame Press, 1996).

31. Dillard, op. cit., pp. 175–76.

32. And I suspect she would concur with at least some of what I have been arguing: "*Self*-consciousness, however, does hinder the experience of the present" (Ibid., p. 81).

33. While God is decidedly important for the *Monadology*, He is not necessary; an atheist metaphysician could simply affirm the monads, and assent that their harmonious interactions were a fact about how the world happens to be. Obviously no atheist could write the *Theodicy*, and the *Discourse* was written largely in defense of the Riccian "Accommodationist" view of how Chinese conversion to the One True Faith could best be effected.

34. After being pressed for weeks by my Chinese graduate students at Fudan in 1982 on how I accounted for the radical differences between the early development of Chinese and Western philosophy, this was my best answer: sophisticated work in arithmetic and geometry preceded the classical period of philosophy in Greece, and followed it in China.

35. Despite my Wittgensteinian predilections, I am reluctant to draw a sharp distinction between so-called "religious" and "nonreligious" language, in the form of "games" or otherwise. Consider the following sentence: "Everyone has duties entailed by the concept of human rights." This seems to fall within the categories of moral, legal, or political discourse (or all three), at least in the West; it is not construed as a religious statement. But "Everyone has duties entailed by the concept of *dharma*" would be seen by most people (again, at least in the West) as a religious statement. What is the difference between the two? For myself, the difference is basically cultural, not conceptual. (See also "Religious and Non-Religious Language, and Propositions About Human Rights" by Jayson A. White; unpublished ms., Ankeny, Iowa.)

36. I have offered critiques of capitalism and the "American way of life" in other writings. Two examples: "On Freedom and Inequality" in *The Aesthetic Turn: Essays Dedicated to Eliot Deutsch*, ed. Roger T. Ames (Open Court Pub. Co., 1999); "Which Rights? Whose Democracy? A Confucian Critique of Modern Western Liberalism" in *Confucian Ethics: A Comparative Study of Self, Autonomy and Community*, ed. K. L. Shun and D. Wong (Cambridge Univ. Press, 2001).

37. A particularly puzzling instance of such a remark was made by Wittgenstein. All of his biographers insist he was a man of the utmost integrity, and scrupulously honest—almost ruthlessly so. They further agree that his life was regularly a tormented one. Yet his final words (cited by Monk, op. cit., p. 411) were "Tell them I've had a happy life." I have pondered this remark often for over three decades now, and still do not know what to make of it.

38. Socrates makes fairly clear his focus on the conceptual rather than the empirical in the *Apology*:

> I must read out their affidavit, so to speak, as though they were my legal accusers: Socrates is guilty of criminal meddling, in that he inquires into things below the earth and in the sky. . . . It runs something like that. You have seen it for yourselves in the play by Aristophanes, where Socrates goes whirling around, proclaiming that he is walking on air, and uttering a great deal of other nonsense about things of which I know nothing whatsoever. I mean no disrespect for such knowledge, if anyone is really versed in it . . . , but the fact is, gentlemen, that I take no interest in it (19 b.–g.).

(*Socrates's Defense*, trans. Hugh Tredennick, in *Plato: Collected Dialogues*, ed. Edith Hamilton and Huntington Cairns [Pantheon Books, Bollingen Series, 1961].) Most of the *Meno* (Ibid.)—as well as other dialogues—is given over to discussions of true opinion on the one hand (the way to Larissa), and to knowledge (of how to double the area of a square) on the other.

39. I would certainly not claim that my reading of Aristotle is a, or the, definitive one, but at least some Greek scholars would, I believe, endorse it. Heath, for example, says:

> In applied mathematics Aristotle recognizes optics and mechanics in addition to astronomy and harmonics. He calls optics, harmonics, and

astronomy the more physical branches of mathematics, and observes that these subjects and mechanics depend for the proofs of their propositions upon the pure mathematical subjects, optics on geometry, mechanics on geometry or stereometry, and harmonics on arithmetic; similarly, he says, *Phaenomena* (that is, observational astronomy) depend on (theoretical) astronomy.

(Sir Thomas Heath, *A History of Greek Mathematics*, vol. I [Dover Publications, 1981], p. 17)

40. Stephen Toulmin, *Cosmopolis* (The Free Press, 1991).

41. Philip Davis and Reuben Hersch, *Descartes' Dream* (Harcourt, Brace, Jovanovich, 1996).

42. The influence of Thomas Kuhn on my thinking about science is obvious, especially as contained in *The Structure of Scientific Revolutions*, 2nd edition (University of Chicago Press, 1967), and in his initial essay and concluding response in I. Lakatos and A. Musgrave, editors, *Criticism and The Growth of Knowledge* (Cambridge University Press, 1970). I must confess, however, that I did not fully appreciate how "wrong" terms in science were nevertheless fruitful until I began reading carefully the detailed entries in the *Dictionary of the History of Science*, edited by W. F. Bynum, E. J. Browne, and Roy Porter (Princeton University Press, 1981) from which several of the details in my narrative have been drawn.

43. This conclusion should not be taken as suggesting that the *Meditations* no longer be read in undergraduate philosophy courses. The work is a classic in the history of Western philosophy, and can be highly useful for getting students to clarify their own thinking about how they conceive "minds" and "bodies." But I do not believe the problem is a real one for professional philosophers, even when it shifts to the concept of consciousness, or zombies, as is currently being done.

44. "Chinese Alchemy and the Manipulation of Time," in *Science and Technology in East Asia*, edited by Nathan Sivin (Science History Publications, 1977), p. 110.

45. I have discussed the benefactor-beneficiary nature of Confucian roles in a number of places, including *A Chinese Mirror* (Open Court Pub. Co., 1991), the "Interlude" chapter.

46. Nathan Sivin, "State, Cosmos, and Body in China," in *Traditional Medicine in Contemporary China* (Center for Chinese Studies, University of Michigan Press, 1987).

47. Some recent work in the neurosciences is suggesting that this ancient Confucian concept of the *xin* may be appropriate for scientific inquiry. See, for example, *Philosophy In the Flesh* by George Lakoff and Mark Johnson (Basic Books, 1999), or *Descartes' Error* by Antonio D'Amasio (G.P. Putnam, 1994).

48. Grace M. Jantzen, *Julian of Norwich* (Paulist Press, 1987).

49. Schuon, op. cit., has argued well for these readings.

50. For a fuller account of this theme, see my "Tracing a Path of Spiritual Progress in the *Analects*" in *Confucian Spirituality*, edited by Mary Evelyn Tucker and Tu Weiming (Crossroads Press, 2001), and in condensed form, in the "Introduction" to the translation of the *Analects* by Roger Ames and me (op. cit.).

51. There are manifold references to the *junzi* in the *Analects* that bear on these themes: 1.2, 4.5, 4.9, 4.10, 4.16, 7.33, 8.7, 12.5, 13.23, 15.9, 15.21, 17.4, 18.7—and many more.

52. While far too many contemporary Western philosophers continue to simply ignore non-Western thought, Arthur Danto has at least attempted to justify that ignorance by claiming that the moral traditions of Asia can have no purchase on us because the moral claims are all justified by appeals to metaphysical views which cannot be credited in our contemporary world (*Mysticism and Morality*, Columbia Univ. Press, 1976). Yet this seems to be little more than a case of special pleading, for while Danto, to his credit, exempts Confucianism from his argument, he nowhere suggests that it is worthy of our serious attention.

THE INSTITUTE
FOR WORLD RELIGIONS

With the understanding that spiritual values are central to the human experience, the Institute for World Religions exists to advance mutual understanding among the world's spiritual traditions. The Institute for World Religions facilitates shared inquiry into the founding visions of the world's faiths so that all might learn from the others' strengths while preserving the integrity of their own.

The Institute for World Religions is also committed to providing an open forum where clergy, theologians, philosophers, scientists, educators, and individuals from a wide variety of disciplines can examine the role of religion in a modern world. All of the Institute's activities take place in an atmosphere of mutual respect and promote the universal human capacity for goodness and wisdom.

Established in 1976, the Institute was the direct result of the inspiration and planning of the Buddhist

Ch'an Patriarch Hsüan Hua and Roman Catholic Cardinal Yu-Bin. Both of these distinguished international leaders in religion and education believed that harmony among the world's religions is an indispensable prerequisite for a just and peaceful world. Each shared the conviction that every religion should affirm humanity's common bonds and rise above narrow sectarian differences.

In keeping with its mission, the Institute offers programs designed to bring the major religious traditions together in discourse with each other and with the contemporary world. Its proximity to the University of California at Berkeley, Stanford University, the Graduate Theological Union, and the rich academic, religious, and cultural environment of the San Francisco Bay area provides an ideal environment for the Institute's programs.

INDEX